About the Author

Catherine Robinson Brown is an avid learner who enjoys reading and writing about love and relationships. She enjoys spending time with her family and friends, walking the hills and trails of her neighborhood with her dog, Storm. *My Path to Infidelity* is her first piece of creative non-fiction.

My Path to Infidelity

Catherine Robinson Brown

My Path to Infidelity

Olympia Publishers
London

www.olympiapublishers.com
OLYMPIA PAPERBACK EDITION

Copyright © Catherine Robinson Brown 2024

The right of Catherine Robinson Brown to be identified as author of this work has been asserted in accordance with sections 77 and 78 of the Copyright, Designs and Patents Act 1988.

All Rights Reserved

No reproduction, copy or transmission of this publication may be made without written permission.
No paragraph of this publication may be reproduced, copied or transmitted save with the written permission of the publisher, or in accordance with the provisions of the Copyright Act 1956 (as amended).

Any person who commits any unauthorized act in relation to this publication may be liable to criminal prosecution and civil claims for damage.

A CIP catalogue record for this title is available from the British Library.

ISBN: 978-1-80074-938-2

This is a work of creative non-fiction. The author has tried her best to recreate events, locations, and conversations from her memories of them. To protect people's privacy, she has changed timelines, the names of individuals and places, identifying characteristics and details such as physical features, occupations, and places of residence.

First Published in 2024

Olympia Publishers
Tallis House
2 Tallis Street
London
EC4Y 0AB
Printed in Great Britain

Dedication

To my soulmate: Thank you for endless love, depths unknown, strength that never fails, comfort that provides warmth, thoughts that provokes dreams, and hope for our tomorrow.

To all women who accept their existence and live in fear of the unknown.
– Kate

Acknowledgments

I never dreamed that I would draft this book, and I certainly never believed that I would share my most personal struggles with others. I have learned that light is the only way to dispel the darkness. We shine brightest when we humble ourselves and ask for forgiveness.

I owe many thanks to many people. To my Lord and Savior, thank you, for your grace and mercy upon my life, for walking with me every day, and offering comfort. To the priests and staff at the Mercy Home for Boys and Girls in Chicago, for support and encouragement through the weekly mass, I am forever grateful.

I would like to thank Olympia Publishers for allowing me the privilege of sharing my story, and Writers NL for your kindness and assistance in helping me edit and shape my story.

To the talented musicians and artists around the world who share their lyrics, notes, and art, thank you for sharing your gifts. Expressing your emotions through song brings comfort to people across the world.

To those who are starving and struggling, I wish I had the means to feed and comfort you all. If I could, I would.

To those who read my book, thank you for giving me your time and attempting to understand me.

Anything is possible if you believe in yourself. Never stop loving, searching, growing, learning, or trying to be a better version of the person you were yesterday.

Be kind and loving, your one act of kindness can travel many miles.

– Kate

True Love

I feel your body, cocooned with mine,
Just being, savoring,
Sharing the same space, breathing the same air,
Not physically joined, yet one,
Souls knit, inseparably,
Not needing to ask to go further,
The answer written large, in the entire sense of togetherness,
My mind reels,
Unable to pull away from heavenly touch and
Thoughts that swirl, and fill and spill,
Filled, full,
What more can I say, what more need I say,
Because you know this, just as sure as me,
It is yours, as much as it is mine,
If there is even a 'you' and a 'me,'
Conjoined, one, in completeness,
Held in my soul for eternity.
– Kate

Foreword

It is my privilege to write a few words as a foreword to this author's first manuscript. I have known the author for some time. We met in unusual circumstances and have shared many hours of deep conversation. As we chatted, the idea of a manuscript based on a very frank account of a life less ordinary came into being. It isn't often such a soul-baring story is told, but that is, in essence, what it is. A journey with many twists and turns, a journey into the unknown, a journey that many will be able to identify with at one level or another. Whether coming from the same continent or from somewhere completely different, this journey spans generations and bridges cultures. It is a journey that touches us all. May you find that it resonates with you as it did with me.

– Connor

Preface

In 2016, my life turned upside down by a host of events and circumstances that were outside of my control. During that year, and the years that followed, a part of me died. There was no returning to the "old me." The trauma that I had endured during those years permanently changed me.

No matter who you are, life transforms you. Sometimes, you may be caught in the current, other times you find yourself in the riptides. Regardless of where you are, the steady lap of the water eventually erodes even the hardest and sharpest of rocks.

My life is complicated. It has been riddled with problems, things I had no control over, and a host of decisions that have profoundly affected me. What you will read will be confusing, heartbreaking, and at times, frustrating, as I bare my soul and share the truth of my life.

I make no apologies for the contradictions, confusion, repetition, and anguish that exist throughout this story. They are a real reflection of the emotions and thoughts that I experienced when I was lost, traumatized, and seeking clarity and solace in my darkest moments.

As a woman who loves deeply and passionately, it is extremely uncomfortable to tell my story of pain and betrayal; I do not want to be judged for my decisions and life choices. I can assure you, no one is harder on me than I am. Life brings circumstances we cannot control or predict, and it is in those times that the unimaginable and unpredictable happens.

Chapter 1

The Trauma – May 2016

I stared forward blankly as the ambulance pulled away from the two-story house that had been my home for the past five years. It was a beautiful home, newly built, with black shingles, blue siding, and an overhanging porch with white railing. Externally, it was perfect, a picturesque home in a family-friendly neighborhood.

Unlike the love-filled home of my youth, this home was filled with anxiety and nervous tension. Most of my time there had been spent walking on eggshells, trying to please and calm the man that I had married. As the sirens wailed, the sound rising and falling slowly in pitch, my mind was focused on the young man it was transporting – my youngest child, James.

James was a handsome, healthy fourteen-year-old boy filled with energy, kindness, and enthusiasm. His smile would light up a room. We shared many of the same personality traits: perseverance, positivity, drive, determination; traits he would need to get him through this ordeal.

Everything had been normal as we'd said goodnight and chatted about our day the night before. But, like most things in my life, normal would not be present for long. I was blissfully unaware of what the next twenty-four hours would hold as I drifted off to sleep.

It seemed like I had closed my eyes for only a minute when

the sound of James crying startled me awake. I quickly jumped from the bed and ran to his room as Liam, my husband, lay snoring loudly. I opened the door to his room and turned on the lights. Sports awards, medals, and memorabilia filled the walls; his desk brightly lit from the gaming keyboard as it changed colors from blue and orange to pink and yellow.

I was fretting when I arrived at his bedside, and asked nervously "What's wrong, sweetheart? Are you not feeling well?"

James sobbed, "Mom, I can't feel my legs and I have a really bad pain in my back."

Panic set in as I tried to determine the context of what he was telling me. I used a pen to jab the soles of his feet, expecting him to recoil in pain, but there was no response. I asked him to stand, but his legs buckled under him. After a few moments of assessment, I offered medication to ease the pain and woke Liam.

"Call for an ambulance, James is paralyzed."

As was Liam's routine, he ignored my plea and huffed and puffed his way to the bedroom, believing I was exaggerating the circumstances. Liam's doubt quickly turned to dismay as he saw his youngest son crying out in pain, lying motionless on his bed.

My heart sank, my pulse quickened, and my mind raced with thoughts of *dear God, what is this?*

I will never forget those horrible fifteen minutes while we waited for the ambulance.

The paramedics arrived, assessed his condition, and decided to transport him to the children's hospital. Unable to determine an immediate diagnosis, they assumed his condition was neurological.

I followed the path of the ambulance, mimicking its movements as it drove slowly over every hump and bump in the road. The breeze from the car window cooled my crimson face and tousled my dyed-blonde hair as I drove, reflecting on the past few years and how much had changed.

I had become a stranger in my own home, unable to be myself, and constantly forced to be mindful of my words and actions. The man I loved was unable to treat me with the care and respect I deserved and desired. I could not reconcile how I had let the mental and emotional abuse go on for so long. I was never the kind of person who would tolerate such behavior.

As I glanced in the rear-view mirror, I wondered what kind of cruelty fate had in store. I was haggard, my complexion like the exterior of an antique vase covered in delicate pink and red roses but filled with tiny cracks. I did not know if I would be able to hold myself together in the face of what was happening.

My blue eyes, heavy from a lack of sleep, looked as deep as the ocean when combined with the bags that had formed under them. I pondered the multiple medical conditions which could have caused James' symptoms and came up empty. In my twenty-five years of working in healthcare, I had never known any similar conditions. My instincts gnawing away at me, I knew whatever was happening was going to be life-changing.

Chapter 2

Mom, Dad, Mya, and Me

Years Earlier
The shadows of my childhood stretched far into the twilight of my adulthood, impacting the choices, decisions, and actions that created and shaped the woman I became. They are as plentiful as a fall harvest, and too numerous to elucidate.

Immersed in the waters of love and engulfed in the fires of expectation, I thrived.

I grew up in a time before the internet, cell phones, and special effects; when respect, honesty, and truth were fashionable. A time when people believed in God and the power of the church was widespread.

My parents were high school sweethearts and, like a teacup, filled to the brim with love for each other.

My mother, a refined woman, was short and plump with coal black hair and brown eyes. She was devoutly Catholic, the dogma and doctrine of the faith engrained in her very being, as well as her daily life. She attended Mass and prayed the rosary regularly.

My father was tall and lean, had a gorgeous smile, pearly white teeth, and dark wavy hair. Like the movie stars of his generation, he was attractive and charismatic.

Unlike my mother, who was blessed to have both her parents, my father, and his siblings, were raised in an orphanage after his father died and his mother was placed in a sanatorium.

Their firstborn child, I was deeply loved and wanted. When I arrived, "dusted in pink powder," my parents believed I was heaven-sent.

In those days, there was no such thing as maternity leave or parental leave, which meant my mother, as breadwinner of the family, worked evening shifts for the extra pay, and Dad worked days as a salesperson.

We lived with my grandparents for the first few months of my life, until my parents purchased their own home a few doors away.

My grandparent's home was on a corner lot. It had a large backyard encompassing the length of half the street. My grandfather had a wood-working shed at the rear of the garden where he would putter and make garden ornaments to mark the walkways, to add depth and beauty to the surroundings.

The garden always felt magical, filled with wonder and beauty. It encouraged the use of imagination with its bright, colorful rose bushes, daffodils, gladioli, raised flower beds, and strawberry and blueberry patches. I was free to roam behind its six-foot walled fence, where nothing and no one could harm me.

Inside, the twelve-foot ceilings and majestic hallways gave the illusion that the sky was the limit.

I remember spending a lot of time in the kitchen, with family, eating and playing. There was a large walk-in pantry and farmhouse sink at one end, a huge woodstove in the middle for cooking and warmth, and a large table opposite the stove where we could all eat together. At the rear of the room were the fridge, cupboards, and buffet for daily dishes. Adjacent to this room was the dining room with fireplace and chandelier. The dining room was reserved for special guests, like the priests who often came for dinner and, later when my grandfather became ill, Sunday

Mass. The table was always set with fine china, crystal glasses, and silver cutlery, adorned with an elegant tablecloth, cotton napkins, and a floral centerpiece.

Next to the dining room was the sitting room to watch television. This room was unique at the time, in that it shared a fireplace with the more formal living room. The large windows brought the outdoors inside, as the sunshine filled the rooms with natural light.

A large mahogany staircase led you to the bedrooms, bathrooms, and loft. It was a four-story home, surrounded by other expensive homes in the center of the city. There was a grocery store, pharmacy, diner, dry cleaner, and park within walking distance, most essential services were located within a single block. Neighbors were well known to each other, though there were few children my age.

My parents, grandparents, aunts, and uncles loved to play with me, especially at my grandparents' house. I would be carried to the top end of the kitchen by my grandparents and placed gently on the floor, while my mother and father would take turns crouching with outstretched arms in front of the kitchen buffet and cupboards, calling out to me.

"Come to Mommy!" "Come to Daddy!"

With squeals of delight and bursts of laughter, I would toddle as fast as I could, most often toward my father, where I would be scooped up, covered in kisses, and hugged tightly. It was there that I felt loved, safe, and untouchable.

When my baby sister, Mya, arrived, I was ecstatic. We shared a room, and our bond grew almost immediately. I did not sleep much when she was a newborn, though, and would frequently call out, "Momma, baba cry" to attract my parents' attention.

Like most children born and raised through the sixties and seventies, we were surrounded by colorful clothes, thoughts, and people. We watched Disney television shows and movies, played with Barbie dolls, and spent a lot of time playing outdoors. We built forts with blankets and lawn chairs, rode our bikes, made mud pies, swam, and played spotlight. There was bright sunshine, laughter, and love in abundance. It was a wonderful time to be a child.

There aren't many stories I recall from my first ten years, just fleeting images of giggles and laughter, and a recollection of being happy.

We lived in a kind of protective bubble, surrounded by family and close friends, rarely mingling with strangers. Although Mom and Dad both came from small families, my uncle married into a family of fourteen, and they quickly became honorary aunts, uncles, and cousins.

People were respectful, mannerly, polite, calm, and hopeful. For the most part, my family prevented us from experiencing any kind of hardship or witnessing anything ugly or controversial.

Time has a way of changing people and circumstances, and somewhere along the way, Mom and Dad's relationship declined. The love that existed when they were first married faded. I would imagine being on opposite shifts, and the lack of time together created a chasm between them.

Mom lived in the black and white world of right and wrong, while Dad always lived in the gray.

When I was ten years old, they separated because Dad was unfaithful.

Unknown to my parents, I had overheard a private conversation when they were discussing the infidelity and dad's departure.

I came inside from playing and I could hear them talking as I climbed the stairs. There was no screaming or yelling, just a civil, cold, matter-of-fact conversation. It was the pitch of my mom's voice and the words being said that caught my attention.

I tip-toed up the stairs until I was close enough to hear clearly. Even at the age of ten I knew enough to know it was not good.

"I want to separate. If you want her, pack your bags, and leave."

Or something like that. I don't recall the exact words, but I remember realizing that my life would never be the same after that moment. It hit me like a bolt of lightning, unexpected and devastating.

I glanced furtively up and down the stairs, as my eyes filled with tears, and ran to my private hiding place to cry. I did not say anything to Mya, the shock was too great, and I was overwhelmed.

As I lay in bed that night, I alternated between staring at the ceiling and Mya. I wondered what would become of me, of our family, without Dad. I wondered how long it would be before Mya learned the truth.

Fortunately, I didn't have to wait long. Mom sat us down the next day and gave us the news.

I cannot recall if she told us about the affair or if I knew because of what I'd overheard, but I realized that Dad had stopped loving Mom and was now with someone else. I also knew that the kisses, hugs, cuddles, and laughter I loved to get from him had come to a screeching halt.

Mya cried like a baby, while I tried to be calm and strong; I was worn out from the crying I had done the night before. I was more interested in what mom was going to say about our future.

"We are still a family, just a little smaller... We all need to be strong and stick together... I love you girls more than anything... nothing will ever change that."

Overall, it went well, until Mya reminded us, through tears, that we had no car and Mom couldn't drive.

"But Mom, how will we get to see Auntie Michelle and Uncle Dennis?"

Kissing our heads, she replied, "Mom will find a way, don't you worry."

It's hard to imagine my ten-year-old self bracing for the future, putting on a suit of armor, but that is the image that has been locked in my head since that day.

The safety and security of Dad's love, and the six-foot fence I had grown accustomed to, was gone.

Mom's words provided comfort to us and let us believe everything would be okay, and, for the most part, time would reveal that she was correct. I never fully understood, at the time, what I had lost or how the effects of that moment would stretch far into the future, to a time I could not foresee, when I would be shaken to my core.

Chapter 3

In Emergency

I parked the car and hurried toward the emergency department. As I entered through the double doors, the smell of antiseptic and hospital cleaners filled my nostrils. I gasped, the smell overwhelming me, as my heart beat heavily in my chest.

The yellow and mint-green walls covered in Disney characters were a pleasant, yet unwelcome, sight. I maneuvered my way through the crowded waiting room to the ambulance bay and stood silently as I watched the ambulance arrive and begin to unload its cargo, James.

Liam had been in the ambulance and walked alongside James on the gurney as he was wheeled into a private room in the Intensive Care Unit.

"Kate, come with me," the nurse directed as she led me to the registration desk.

Once I finished answering the questions that confirmed James' identity, I rushed to his side, inquiring if anything had changed during the ride to the hospital. To my dismay, the symptoms were still occurring. Thankfully, they had not worsened.

I sat by his bedside in a large wingback chair and began googling his symptoms, searching for information so I could ask intelligent questions when the physicians arrived.

Liam and I watched quietly as the medical team performed multiple neurological assessments. Each doctor seemed more stumped than the last, repeatedly asking the same questions to ascertain what was causing the paralysis.

Finally, a neurologist arrived. He was a short-statured man, of East Indian heritage. He carried a merlot-colored bag with a large reflex hammer extending out the side. As he performed a variety of tests using soft Q-tips, sharp pieces of wood, and other neurological tools, I searched James' face for a reaction, but there was none. My son was paralyzed, without reason or cause.

As the neurologist spoke, I could barely comprehend what he was saying; my mind was a million miles away in the medical books that I had studied twenty years ago.

Distracted, I answered his questions to the best of my ability and nodded inconsequentially as he explained his plan and course of treatment. I did not understand the conditions he mentioned, Transverse Myelitis… Guillain Barre… the terms were completely foreign to me. Despite my time working in healthcare, I had never heard of these conditions. As the neurologist returned to the nursing desk, I reached for my cell phone and started googling again.

Transverse Myelitis is a rare neurological condition that affects one in a million each year; Guillain Barre is a rare disorder that affects one in one hundred thousand. My eyes bulged and my heart ceased beating as I read "some never recover."

I shook my head, swearing that this will not happen to him, to us. It was just not possible. God would never allow this to happen to my sweet, innocent boy.

I never, for even a moment, believed that God would fail James or me. He had been steadfast and true my whole life. It did not seem possible that I would have to endure more pain.

I glanced lovingly at James; the medications had eased his discomfort and he was sleeping peacefully. Wrapped in the blue and white hospital sheets, he looked as innocent as the day he was born, with his rose-colored cheeks and crew cut hair sticking off in all directions. He looked healthy, despite his immobile frame. As I watched him sleep, my mind drifted back in time.

James had been a large, healthy baby, born by uncomplicated C-section in the winter of 2002. He had been an angelic, bouncing, bundle of joy with pink coloring and his dad's sweet smile. I had been an older mom when I was pregnant with James, and I had undergone a series of tests to ensure a healthy baby.

During my pregnancy, there had been questions regarding the health of the baby, concerns about diabetes, and the misconception that James was one of twins – turned out he was simply a large baby. He had been an inquisitive child, content and jolly. He'd loved to play and learn and had taken his first steps when he had been only eleven months old.

My pregnancy with James was the opposite of my experience with his brother. William, my firstborn, arrived in the winter of 1999. I remember it well, the thrill of a baby growing inside me; the joy from the first flutters and kicks to the strange shapes my belly would make as the baby flip-flopped to get comfortable. When William had been in my belly, he would sleep with his head down and bum up. His movement had continually made me laugh, stoking my anticipation for his arrival.

Unlike the one-hour labor with James, I had endured forty-four hours of labor with William before they had decided I needed a C-section. William had swallowed amniotic fluid and appeared black in color instead of pink when he was born. This complication results in a baby having difficulty breathing on their own. For the first few hours of his life, William had been in an incubator. Temporarily paralyzed from the epidural, I had been unable to bond with him. It was a horrible experience for a first-time mother. Two entirely different pregnancies for two mildly different sons.

It was not unusual for us to be at the hospital with the boys over the course of their childhoods. William had had surgery on his kidneys as a baby and, over the course of his teenage years, had countless surgeries for issues with his ears and throat.

James had his share of hospitalizations too. When he was an infant, he contracted Respiratory Syncytial Virus (RSV) from our cat. As a preschooler, he had been struck by a car while running away from his babysitter. During elementary school, he had broken his arm while playing cops and robbers with William. James had frequently had sore throats and common colds and had become quite comfortable in the hospital environment. But, this time, I could sense something was terribly amiss.

Liam stared at me, captivated by the activity around us, a look of fear on his face, his eyebrows furrowed and his lips taut. As he stood to stretch his legs, his six-foot frame outlined the muscles he had developed over decades of manual labor. He looked much older than his age; the years of drinking and smoking etched into the lines around his eyes and mouth.

I remained silent and patient, as I glanced casually around the room. There was medical equipment scattered on trolleys and in cupboards, and tubes of every shape and color lay in red and blue bins. Rows of gas nozzles lined the walls; machines beeped with James' heart rate and oxygen readings. There were no other patients sharing the secluded space with us.

It was five a.m. We had already been here for two hours and had no answers. Nurses and doctors were bustling about, treating other patients; some smiled with looks of compassion as they glanced in our direction, others were indifferent as they effectively completed their tasks.

A heavy sigh escaped my lips as I tilted my head backward and closed my eyes for a moment. *Dear Lord, what do you have in store for me now?* I wondered.

Chapter 4

Post Separation

Years Earlier

My childhood circumstances formed the cloth on which the intricacies and complexities of my life were woven, the pattern gradually revealed over time.

The week after my dad left, Mom went to driving school to get her license, contented with our response that the only thing we would miss was a car ride. After three failed attempts, she successfully received her license. My grandfather gave her his old car as a celebratory gift.

Although she was always a nervous driver, the freedom that came with transportation and the ability to see unfamiliar places provided Mya and I with hope and optimism. Life had not changed much; we would be okay in our downsized little family.

Mom drowned us in love, and continually sacrificed her needs and life for ours. She never attempted to foster a meaningful relationship with anyone after her split with Dad. Although she went on a few dates, Dad somehow managed to intercept them, usually making a scene and making her uncomfortable, reducing her desire to try again.

When not working, she spent as much time with us as possible. She took us shopping, to get our hair done, and helped us with our homework. She always had a strong focus on education, and her love of writing was instilled in us through the many speeches, poems, assignments, and essays we wrote together. Over time, Mya, Mom, and I became best friends, sharing our troubles and secrets, laughing, crying, and cussing at the circumstances life would throw at us.

Mom never spoke ill of Dad; she always focused on the positive, choosing to see the good in him. Her love clouded her perception of him, and she frequently pointed out his strengths to us, overlooking the obvious pain he had inflicted on her. She never wanted to paint a negative image of him in our minds.

Her love was unconditional, unwavering, and enduring. We meant the world to her, and she would have done anything to shield us from harm.

Like most single parents, she did everything in her power to fulfil the role of two parents – mentally, emotionally, and financially – including purchasing a cabin as a diversion from the challenges we faced.

As we grew into teenagers, we would board the car on Saturday mornings and head out over the highway to our tiny cabin in the woods. There, we would have fires, roast marshmallows, swim, and walk the train tracks until well past midnight.

It not only provided a sense of freedom for Mya and I, but a distraction from our reality as well. I think it was Mom's way of giving us a different 'six-foot fence,' a new place where we would feel safe and untouchable.

It was difficult, as a child, to understand why my parents had separated and to watch my dad walk away from us. I could never understand that it had nothing to do with me. I suppose, like any child, I wondered what I had done wrong, assuming my arguing with my sister, or some other discretion, had been the cause. I never understood the complexity of their relationship until I was much older.

I loved my father; he always took time for me and made me feel special. I loved coming home after school to play with him or help in the kitchen.

On the days he was tired, Mya and I would frequently get a glass of water and comb his hair while he lay on the couch, relaxing. Sometimes, we would take out our makeup and put lipstick and rouge on him. Other days, he would be the student as Mya and I played teacher, using chalk to mark on the walls and provide him with the lessons we had been taught by our own teachers that day.

As I grew up, I wished Dad had been there to give me guidance on boys – how they think, what they want, what their behavior means. I never fully grasped how profoundly the lack of his influence would affect me. I missed having that male relationship and perspective in my life. The day he left, I felt lost.

His absence created a void that was filled by the strong, independent women in my family.

It was not long after my parents separated that my grandfather became ill with Parkinson's disease. I fondly recall helping my grandmother cook and bake in the kitchen, cutting vegetables for stews and making pie crusts for his favorite desserts. He loved my presence in the house and my willingness to help my grandmother. Most especially, he loved spending time with me, praying, eating, and laughing together. He always sang, "Katie," a war song from 1918, as he tickled me and roared with laughter as I giggled, begging for mercy.

Visits to my grandparents' house diminished over time, as my family tried to protect Mya and I from seeing his rapid decline. Gradually, he started choking while he was eating and, eventually, he could not eat at all. It was truly tragic because he had been a large man who'd loved food. He passed away from starvation two years after his diagnosis.

My grandmother, my great-aunt, and my mother pooled their resources and decided that we needed a fresh start. They moved us from our family home to the opposite end of the city, where we met new friends and began a new life.

Despite coming from a single parent home, Mya and I never lacked anything because our family was quite generous. Mom had a strong family support system, people who brought to life the adage 'it takes a village to raise a child.'

Mom never drank or smoked, wanting to be a pristine example of a good parent for me and Mya. Her focus was on raising young ladies who would not be stigmatized for coming from a single parent home, women who would be respected and admired.

She was not interested in matters she considered trivial. The Catholic faith denounced pride and vanity. Therefore, she rarely commented on my physical appearance, opting, instead, to instill a sense of humility, though I was frequently told by others that I was a 'gorgeous' girl.

Like all children, there are stories from my childhood that I would rather forget. Junior high was a time when I loved school and learning, but other students were often unkind. They made fun of me because I was overweight for my age. I suppose, in hindsight, the departure of my father created a void in my life, and I filled it with junk food.

One time, I found a fellow student in the locker room, wearing my jeans, pulling them out at the waist, mocking me. I was furious. I savagely grabbed her arm, ferociously saying, "If I ever catch you doing this again, you will be sorry." Horrified with myself and extremely hurt by her actions, I went home crying.

Upon reflection, I am shocked that I had the courage to stand up for myself. I was such a sensitive soul, I loved so freely and willingly, that I could not comprehend why she or anyone else would want to hurt me. Left with deep emotional wounds from this encounter, I became shy and withdrawn.

That was probably when the body image issues began and they continued well into my forties. I never had confidence in myself or my appearance, and I wasted a lot of time being on diets, trying to lose weight, and comparing myself to others. My mind interpreted slimmer people as better people. This was not true, of course, but it was the way in which I saw the world.

The fashion magazines I frequently read were filled with pictures of super thin models leading fabulous lives, propagating the belief that I could not compete and was less than par.

For as long as I can remember, I was twenty to thirty pounds overweight. I grew up in the generation of Pepsi, chocolate, and potato chips, and I relished them. My breakfast choice when I was a teenager consisted of a tall glass of Pepsi on ice and a piece of homemade chocolate cake. Talk about the breakfast of champions! I had no understanding of the fact that food played such a significant role in my appearance, or of the importance of a healthy diet and exercise.

I did not look like the models on the magazine covers, and so, in my mind, I needed to lose weight. As I got older, I tried dieting. During one successful dieting episode, I lost twenty pounds, bought a new outfit, and went to school, beaming, proud of my accomplishment.

One of my classmates, whose opinion I valued, sabotaged my weight loss plan. "Wow, you look good. Now, if you could lose another twenty pounds, you would look *great*!" As she spoke, I slumped in my chair, my heart broken, my spirit crushed. No matter what I did, it never seemed sufficient for anyone.

Believing that I could never compete or meet acceptable social standards, I stopped dieting that day, and my weight gradually escalated again.

I was tired of comparing myself to others, of seeking acceptance that never came; tired of trying to live up to unreasonable expectations and trying to please everyone. I should have been focused on pleasing myself, but I did not have that mindset.

For the first twenty years of my life, Mom made most decisions for me. I seemed unable to convince her that I could make appropriate choices. Because of this, I had little to no opportunity to make decisions for myself or deal with the consequences of any decision I made. To make matters worse, we were frequently at odds over what constituted the "right" decision.

To this day, I do not know why she acted like this. Did she think I was incompetent? Or was she just so used to being in control that she feared any outcome other than the one she anticipated?

Assuming I would simply 'do as I was told' caused conflicting emotions. I was grateful for not having to make the decisions, but angry because I could not make them.

My family presumed that I would follow the same path as my mother. They reminded me daily of the importance of getting an education, being a lady, and being a virgin. There never seemed to be any consideration for changing times and culture, as if we were stuck in the 1950s, an era where children followed their parents' instruction without question.

They clearly defined the path ahead of me, not realizing that

I did not agree with any of it.

I was adamant that I had to be independent. Eventually, my mother gave me the power to create and be responsible for my own future, encouraging and ensuring my formal education. It was the best gift she ever gave me, and the strongest building block in my personal foundation.

My university life was uneventful. I chose a wide swath of courses to determine my interests and future career. I had little time for socializing or partying, and the couple of dormitory dances that I did attend were ruined either by my mom or by alcohol.

One night, after finishing exams, I went to the local university bar, Kelly's Pub, to celebrate. To be honest, my friends and I went to get drunk (may as well call it what it was). I was looking forward to unwinding and relaxing after the extensive hours of studying I had completed.

Dressed alike in jeans and shirts with floral prints – the ultimate in fashion in those days – we were an attractive group of young ladies. We had received the first round of drinks and were sitting with several prospective male colleagues when campus security staff arrived and headed straight for our table.

While I was a student, I worked with, and developed a close friendship with, security staff. They serviced both the hospital and the university, and we frequently crossed paths. I assumed they were coming to tease us or join in the fun, but I was mistaken. They informed me that my mother had called, requested they locate me, and inform me she had accepted an overnight shift for me at the hospital and had assured the supervisor I would report as scheduled.

I was outraged! *How could she do this to me*? I wanted and

needed some downtime, but I had to pack up my belongings and head for home to get some rest before the shift started.

This kind of behavior was not unusual for Mom. It felt like she controlled every aspect of my life and, out of respect, I never rebelled.

On another night out, I decided to be adventurous. I did not enjoy beer or wine; my alcoholic preference was sweet drinks – peach schnapps and orange juice or Singapore slings. I decided to change things up and sample lemon gin and lime. It was a nice drink, not too sweet, but, also, not the kind of drink you should indulge in when scheduled to work in the early morning.

We lingered at the dance with our friends until four a.m. My sister and one of our friends wondered how they were going to get me into the car. The challenge increased when they tried to get me into my bed. I had a waterbed, a sloshy, bouncy, bubbly, *moving* waterbed. That was the first and only night I did not love it. The room was spinning, the bed was swaying, and my head was exploding.

Oh God, make it stop! Please stop everything from spinning round and round, I thought. I was nauseous.

"Mya, help me!" I cried.

"Put your foot out over the bed," she answered.

It did not work.

"Put the other one out," she hollered.

Oh, God, that made it worse! The room continued to spin; my stomach continued to churn.

I do not know when I finally fell asleep, I just know that I was not asleep long when the alarm went off at seven a.m. I was queasy and hungover. It was time to get my shower and go to work.

Mom forbade calling in sick. A commitment made must be

honored. She slammed the cupboard doors loudly, the noise reverberating in my head. This was her method to ensure I would not forget my actions and make the mistake of wanting to repeat them. Oh, my! I should have told her she had no fear of an incident like this repeating itself. It was the worst headache I had ever experienced. I never, ever drank lemon gin and lime again.

Mom believed earning my own money would instill an excellent work ethic in me. She funded the tuition and books for the first year of university, but the remaining costs were my responsibility.

As university costs increased, my minimum wage jobs were not making ends meet. Fortunately, there were summer relief positions available in healthcare and the rate of pay was significantly higher than the wages to which I was accustomed.

While the work was interesting, the shifts were awful. I occasionally had to work an overnight shift and found them exceedingly difficult.

I was a girl who needed a lot of sleep to function, and sleeping when you were supposed to be awake and awake when the rest of the world was sleeping was horrid. I adjusted, though I prayed never to have to do them again.

Life is full of sacrifices like these; to teach us compassion, empathy, and sympathy. Thankfully, I learned those lessons early in my career, and I grew to appreciate those who sacrificed their sleep, and their personal lives, to care for others.

Working in a union-based environment while attending university presented an opportunity to progress, build seniority, and gain permanent full-time employment. It took five long years of toiling shift work in multiple departments before I achieved permanent status in Support Services.

My first position was as an administrative assistant, pulling reports and filing information. Luckily, the department had a hierarchical structure, with opportunities for advancement to specialty positions, such as technician, supervisor, and manager.

Passionate for knowledge, I took advantage of every course that was offered. When an opportunity for progression arose, I would be ready.

Work provided a means to get the recognition and acceptance I desperately craved, and the validation I was constantly seeking. I excelled in every position I undertook and, years later, evolved into a well-respected manager.

After five years of university, I graduated and received my bachelor's degree. Mom cried, she was so proud of me; I cried, feeling I had wasted the last five years of my life.

Though I was proud of my accomplishment, I didn't believe I was any further ahead. I was not about to launch a successful career like other graduates because I did not have a career path in mind. I had a piece of paper that meant something to my mother. I yearned for something to challenge and stimulate my mind, and this was not it.

Chapter 5

The Diagnosis – 2016

Startled by an alarm, my eyes popped open. For a moment, I was disoriented, until I noticed that the alarm indicated that the bag of IV fluids had emptied. Hours had passed since we'd arrived at the hospital, and I realized I now had calls to make. James was still sleeping soundly. Liam was nowhere in sight. *Unsurprising*, I thought, but pushed the thought out of my mind. This was no time to be concerned with his behavior.

My first call was to Mya. I often referred to my sister as the family coordinator because she took charge and coordinated all calls, social events, and information for the entire family. Her knowledge of the events that were transpiring would save me a ton of phone calls. After a couple of unsuccessful attempts to reach her by phone, I decided to send a text. *I am in the children's emergency department. James is paralyzed*, it read. Simple and to the point.

The second call was to my boss, advising him that I would be absent for the next few days until we could determine James' diagnosis and prognosis. Shocked, he requested I stay in touch and provide regular updates.

Mom, a known hypochondriac and incessant worrier, was next, and I dreaded to place the call. I decided to relay as few details as possible to allay her fears.

As I conveyed the little information we had, I could hear her choke out the words, "I will pray." I thanked her for her prayers and offered as much hope as I could, knowing that James' prognosis was as uncertain as the weather on the Canadian east coast.

Dad, I texted; he was more technologically savvy, and I knew he'd be more understanding of my need for peace during this worrisome time.

Within minutes, I could feel the vibration of my phone in my pocket. I glanced at the caller identification; it was Mya. I tried to speak calmly, explaining what had happened and the titbits of information I had at my disposal.

There was no definitive diagnosis, and more testing would be conducted. As I was speaking, Liam appeared with hot beverages – thank goodness, I needed something to awaken and sustain me.

I had barely enjoyed a few sips of my tea when the porters arrived to bring James for a CT scan to check for anomalies in his brain and spinal cord. I collected our belongings, and Liam and I followed the staff down the long, empty hallways to the Diagnostic Imaging department.

The old wooden chair, covered in a mustard yellow material from a previous decade, creaked loudly as I sat down and leaned back. Unable to enter the MRI room, I sat, crossing and uncrossing my legs, fidgeting with my hands; Liam paced back and forth, wearing a path in the gray floor. It was unnerving to not be in the room to hold James' hand, to offer comfort and reassurance.

While we waited anxiously for the results of the scan, I responded to the multiple texts popping up on my screen as word of James' condition spread.

When I raised my eyes, Amelia, my best friend, was standing

in front of me. Her white nurse's uniform was in stark contrast to her caramel complexion, outlining her petite facial features and short stature.

'What is going on?"

As I relayed the information I had received from the neurologist, Mya appeared.

We sat together, googling the medical conditions, trying to determine which would be the better diagnosis for James.

As we chatted amongst ourselves, Amelia's voice echoed in my head, "let's pray for this, and hope for that."

I paused, as my voice quavered, "I am thanking God he is alive. I can comfort him, kiss him, hug him, and hear his voice. That is a blessing, I cannot ask for more. He is in God's hands, and I trust He will get us through this." Everyone went silent, they knew I was right.

When the scan was finished, I asked Amelia to speak with the physician to obtain the results. She could communicate with medical terms that I would not understand, and hopefully gain a better perspective. We sat together, as a family, waiting for the neurologist to return.

The physician's somber expression was the first indication that the results were not favorable. As the words flowed from his lips, the air was sucked out of my lungs and the adrenaline surged through my body. I could not think straight, my mind unable to absorb the diagnosis. I inhaled deeply, trying to catch my breath.

James had Transverse Myelitis. He would be admitted to the hospital, and treatment would begin immediately, in hope of reversing the damage.

My sweet baby might never recover; the unthinkable had become reality.

Chapter 6

Love?

Thirty Years Earlier

Love – thousands have tried to explain and define it, without success. There are many types of love, and degrees of love, and most of us, from an early age, seek to find the epitome of love in ourselves or in another.

Isn't it strange how love is never as we learn it to be? In hindsight, I had no idea what love was. Not. A. Clue. As a practical person, part of me knew that it was not like that portrayed in the movies, but I did not really have a gauge as to how different it would be.

I do not feel like I ever really dated, at least not in the typical sense, where a boy calls and invites you to dinner or a movie. That never happened to me.

My distorted self-perception convinced me it was because I was overweight and unattractive. I dressed well, acted confident and jovial, but I was pretending. I was friendly, smiled a lot, greeted everyone I met with a bubbly, "hello," but it did not seem to matter.

I met Pat, my first long term boyfriend, when I was recruited by a modelling agency to model plus size women's clothing in the local mall.

We had mutual acquaintances at the time and ran into each other after a modelling show, where my friend introduced us. Pat was an average-looking guy with brown hair and blue eyes. After our first meeting, he told my friend that he was head over heels in love with me.

Pat and I dated for five years. We spent a lot of our time together with friends; camping, walking, and in the winter, snowmobiling and skating. We did not argue much, primarily because I was such an agreeable person.

Mom, a virgin when she married, repeatedly preached the "save yourself for marriage" speech, and routinely attempted to function as my chastity belt. She lay on the Catholic guilt so thick that I was terrified to have sex, afraid of getting pregnant or contracting a sexually transmitted infection.

Ultimately, I ignored her, and when I turned nineteen, he took my virginity.

Like many first loves, Pat and I eventually drifted apart. As we grew, life brought us in different directions. I was focused on my education; he was focused on marriage. The timing was off; I was not prepared to be a mother at twenty, and I wanted a solid career and income before children came along. Once he cheated, the relationship ended.

Wounded, I was unable to understand the reason for his betrayal and blamed myself, assuming it was something I had done wrong. I had given him my virginity in anticipation of a future together, and that future disappeared six months later. This impacted me greatly and a voice in my head whispered that I was not enough.

I cried for a week, nonstop, every night. I thought Mya was going to kill me. We still shared a room at the time, my incessant sobbing kept her awake, and her pillows were not thick enough to drown out the noise.

I could not figure out what the other girl had that I did not.

Bigger breasts? Better kisses? A higher IQ?

It stung, making me resentful and bitter, and filling me with feelings of inadequacy. It was months before I felt like myself again.

With my heart maimed and scarred, I buried the pain and the memories, and tried to move forward.

Seeking to fill the void of loneliness after Pat and I broke up, I would frequent the local bars during the summer months. Not to drink, but to dance and flirt with men in the hope of meeting a man with whom I could have a long-term relationship and eventually marry.

One night, I met a gorgeous police officer named Greg. He was tall and thin, with a great body, dark hair, white teeth, and an inviting smile. He was lean and muscular; his shirt accentuated his wide shoulders, and his jeans highlighted his firm bum. Based on our conversations, he appeared intelligent and charming.

Greg treated me with respect and dignity. I really liked him, and I felt good about myself when I was with him. After dating for a few weeks, I brought him home to meet Mom. He was stable, with a good career, and I knew this was the kind of man Mom would find acceptable as a potential husband. As they chatted, he expressed his delight in having met me, declaring that I was amazing, and he could not believe girls like me existed.

I beamed and thought, *Wow! He really likes me!* I was filled with hope and excitement, thinking I had brought home a man who met Mom's standards and with whom I could have a future.

I did not have time to decide if I was going to give Greg my heart. The following weekend, he married his pregnant girlfriend and I never heard from him again. I was shocked and utterly disillusioned.

What the heck? Why didn't he tell me? Was I some final attempt at sex before marriage?

It made me more confused than I already was; more doubtful, skeptical, and fearful that there was something wrong with me. Another battle wound. Again, the voices in my head screamed I was not enough.

Months later, when we crossed paths in a local bar, I just glared at him, while he stared somberly in my direction. We have not spoken from that day to this.

Another failed relationship, another round of blaming myself and examining the million possibilities of what I could have done wrong.

I often speculated that he was dating me because of issues with illegal drugs at the house next door to mine; investigating our involvement, as part of his job. Had he asked, I would have explained that I hated anything to do with drugs.

The following summer, my friend introduced me to her cousin who was in the army. We went to dinner, a movie, and for a relaxing drive. We stopped in a quiet country location and, as I was in mid conversation, he came across the seat and was kissing me in less than thirty seconds. Oblivious to his intentions, he scared me so much that I got a massive nosebleed.

I frantically searched for a way to stop the blood from getting on my white T-shirt dress, trying not to look like the victim of a car wreck. I cringed at the thought of attempting to explain the bloody dress to my mother.

Cupping my hands together, I attempted to catch most of the blood, while he rummaged through the car for towels, tissues, or something to help the situation. There was nothing – no napkins, towels, or paper. My mind raced to find a solution. All that came to my mind was a sanitary napkin in my purse.

Embarrassed and still in shock, I asked him to hand it to me. Like the blood, I was bright red. Mortified. A few minutes later, we drove to the nearest washroom, and I washed the remaining blood off my hands before he took me home. Regardless of the embarrassment, the sanitary napkin was effective. As expected, we never went out again.

After those shenanigans, I did not date anyone for a long time. A *long* time. I could not bring myself to try. I had myself convinced that I simply was not enough for any man, and I doubted my self-worth. I began to feel invisible and unimportant, doubting that love was in the cards for me at all.

Chapter 7

Losing Amanda – March 2016

Stunned from the diagnosis and the uncertainty of the future, my thoughts drifted back in time, reliving the events of the past four months. The year that had begun slowly and easily, had quickly changed tempo. Life was speeding along like a freight train, and I was holding on by my fingernails.

2016 had begun like any other year, filled with excitement and eager anticipation of the year to come. I was engrossed in the fantasy that my family was happy, my life perfectly normal.

At the beginning of the year, Liam and I purchased a new vehicle to transport the boys to their sports games and extracurricular activities. William had begun dating; James was planning a school trip to France.

Our home was a hub of activity, filled with friends of the boys who had become like my own children.

As a mother, it thrilled me to watch my sons learn about love and experience their first romantic relationships. I loved the glow on their faces as they told their stories and teased each other.

William introduced us to Amanda in the fall of 2014. An incredibly beautiful girl with long, dark, wavy hair, she had a captivating smile, petite facial features, sparkling eyes, and plump, full lips. Her tall, shapely frame complemented her striking appearance.

She was intelligent and doing well in school, though she had a lot of responsibilities at home for a sixteen-year-old. I would often hear her speak of staying up late to care for her younger sisters and brothers, bathing and feeding them well past bedtime, despite having to go to school the next day.

William and Amanda shared a mutual love and respect for each other. William was blessed with the gift of kindness, and genuinely concerned for people. He had an ability to sense a person's need for love and guidance, a trait he inherited from me. I believe that was his attraction to Amanda.

They studied at our home on many occasions, and each time she was there, I could see something was awry, though I could never quite put my finger on it. Amanda frequently appeared on edge and jittery. I was never certain if it was because she was shy and introverted, if our presence made her uncomfortable, or if there was more going on which could not be readily seen.

Late one evening, in the summer of 2015, while they were studying, I told William that it was time for Amanda to go home.

William replied, "Mom, she can't go home. She is afraid her mom will beat her."

"What do you mean?" I asked.

As he explained her situation, I was horrified. Whenever Amanda did not do as requested, her mom would unleash her anger, striking out physically and emotionally.

My motherly instincts erupted from within to protect this innocent child from such horror. I called social workers seeking advice, brought her to the emergency room in search of assistance to address the abuse, and eventually returned to my home to rest. Consultations with doctors, social workers, and friends, uncovered the worst. Legally, I was not allowed to keep her with me because she was too young to give consent. Genuinely concerned for her safety, I wrestled with what to do for this young girl that I had grown to love as my own.

The next morning, her mom called to collect her, and Amanda cried, fearful of what she would face when she returned home. I comforted her in my arms, stroking her hair to calm and soothe her, reassuring her that it would be okay because she no longer had to face this alone.

We discussed an escape plan for Amanda in the event her worst fears came true. If there were indications her mom was going to lash out, she was to run out of the house and call me. We would meet at our predetermined location, and I would call the police enroute.

As the car pulled away from our home, I cringed, overwhelmed with panic and concern for this young, innocent girl.

I paced anxiously around the kitchen, clanking pots and pans, fiddling with dishes, wringing my wrinkled, water-soaked hands, wondering what was transpiring. Time seemed to stand still until, finally, thirty minutes later, the phone rang, and I rushed to answer it.

The caller identified himself as Mr. Smith, Amanda's neighbor, who, in a gruff voice, asked to speak with Mrs. Brown. He told me that he had witnessed a domestic disturbance and a young girl in need of assistance. Amanda requested he call me to assure me she was safe with him and his wife, and to inform me that he had called the police.

Mr. Smith had witnessed Amanda come screaming out of the house in tears as her mother was clawing at her, trying to get her inside, leaving long cat-like scratch marks on her face and neck. At that moment, he had intervened, physically prying her from the arms of her mother.

He assured me that the authorities had arrived, secured

Amanda in their vehicle, and were transporting her to the hospital. I thanked him for calling and left my home immediately to meet them there.

I waited patiently as the nurses and doctors assessed her condition and took pictures of her injuries. The emergency room physician consulted with Amanda and declared her an emancipated minor – this was the legal leverage I needed to bring her home with me.

As we walked slowly to the car, we realized that she had nothing but the clothes on her back and the medication given to her by the doctors. I called my friends, who graciously gave clothes, shoes, and a coat to get her through the next couple of days.

On the way home, we stopped to purchase underwear, toiletries, and other necessities she would need. During the weeks that followed, we made several trips to the local mall, where I purchased clothes until her closet and dresser drawers were full.

As we navigated through the formal process, social workers became involved, and we agreed to a permanent arrangement. We worked together to ensure that we completed every request, so that Amanda would not fall through the cracks of the system.

Uncertain of her future, I often saw Amanda lost in thought, gazing off into space. She appeared to be unaccustomed to the overwhelming love I offered and unfamiliar with how to be a young, carefree teenager. Although she no longer had to help raise her siblings, she was concerned for their safety as they remained at home while social workers investigated the allegations of abuse.

Once the mountain of responsibilities was lifted off her shoulders, she was unsure how to adapt to this new existence. On one occasion, she innocently asked, "How long will it be like this?"

I smiled at her, recognizing that she was unaccustomed to the freedom to be herself. "It will always be like this, honey. You can relax and be yourself. Take time for you – do your homework, study, have a bubble bath, or go out with friends. Your time is your own."

She looked at me as if I had three heads, completely unsure that this new life was real.

We renovated the basement, building her a bedroom to make her feel part of the family. We gave her office space, to do homework, and a TV area, to unwind and relax. Like mother and daughter, Amanda and I shopped together to choose her paint color, flooring, bedroom furniture, bedding, curtains, and lamps.

We purchased a computer for her to do homework, and a cell phone to contact us in times of trouble. I made sure she always had pocket money to join her friends for lunch or go out after school. I did everything in my power to give her what she desired and needed.

I brought her to a dentist to have her cavities filled and teeth fixed, an eye specialist for her glasses, and to our family doctor for the medication she required. We visited physicians to help heal the abuse, and counsellors for rehabilitation. I attended meetings, appointments, and therapy sessions with her to offer support. I wanted to demonstrate how much I cared. She was the daughter I had never had and had always wanted, and my only wish was to love and heal her.

While we tried to adjust as a family, there were complications and growing pains. She was William's girlfriend, which meant that we had to keep a close eye on the time they spent together. I did not want them having sex in my home, and I definitely did not want Amanda to become pregnant. I was trying to help shape her life, not complicate it. I knew it would be difficult for William to accept having her as his sibling instead of his girlfriend, and vice versa, so we opted for a slow and smooth transition.

Despite the turmoil, things seemed calm and settled, at least for six or seven months. Once William had accepted Amanda as his sibling, he broke up with her. The sense of peace that had existed in our home became non-existent when William introduced his new girlfriend, Sarah, a few months later.

Tall, blonde, and beautiful, Sarah was a great fit for William. She was pursuing her formal education, and her family background was similar to mine. She was quiet and polite, and we welcomed her into our home.

Amanda, understandably, was not pleased with this turn of events. She had not adjusted to her new surroundings or family, let alone the loss of William, and began acting out. She would lock William out of the house if she arrived home from school first, throw icy water on him when he was in the shower, and text him during school hours with the intention of getting him in trouble. She was angry with him for breaking up with her, and fearful of what this meant for her and the living arrangements.

Of course, I did not learn about any of this until months later. If I had known, I would have supported my son and dealt with the issue in a kind and loving manner, quelling Amanda's fears while offering reassurance of her living arrangements. I wanted her to have a positive, happy future, but fate had a different plan.

The prescribed medication did not seem to be sufficient for her needs and, without my knowledge, she was purchasing more of it on the street. I never understood why; if she had asked, I would have returned to the physician and discussed a dosage change.

To pay for the street medication, one of Amanda's friends gained access to my jewelry box and sold all the contents. These were treasures that I had collected from birth to adulthood; necklaces, bracelets, and rings that were gifts from my parents, family, and friends. They sold my father's wedding band, my grandmother's family heirloom ring, and rings I had collected from around the world, which were priceless to me because of the memories associated with them. Gifts from people I would never see again, who had passed on and left me their most valuable treasures, gifts of sentimental and inestimable value. I was heartbroken and utterly devastated.

Angry, I confronted her and demanded an explanation. Unable to provide an acceptable reason, she apologized, saying she did not mean to cause issues. As I stared into her troubled face, my heart softened; I could not blame her, she needed help. I could not determine an appropriate punishment for such an act as there was no means to retrieve the priceless items; I had lost them forever.

Seeing my anger made her uncomfortable. All she had seen from me, up to this point, was a kind and loving mother, who offered unconditional love and acceptance. Uncertain how to respond, she requested to leave.

Hastily, I replied, "Fine, pack your things."

We filled our vehicle with her belongings and headed toward her extended family. As we drove, I stared at her in the rear-view mirror.

Crying, she texted me, "I am sorry. Please forgive me. I do not want to be alone."

My heart ached as I read it, and I asked Liam to turn around, thinking we could try again. I remembered her appointment with her doctor and knew she needed to attend. We had been on a waiting list for a long time; I could not in good conscience let her miss it when it was critical to her health and recovery.

We headed home and unpacked the truck, but the air was filled with constant tension and uncertainty. A week later, we met with the physician to discuss her issues, but our relationship had changed, and nothing felt the same. There was a sense of uneasiness and a lack of trust, and the bond I thought we had created faded.

Her behavior was part of the cycle of abuse, as I later learned in therapy.

The four-stage cycle is used to describe the way abuse occurs in relationships. The stages – tension, incident, reconciliation, and calm – continuously repeat themselves.

It works like this: tension builds between the abuser and victim when the abuser lashes out in response to external stressors.

The victim tries to appease the abuser to prevent the abuse from happening, which increases their anxiety.

The abuser, unable to cope with stress, releases their tension on the victim, attempting to gain power and control by name calling, violence, threats of harm, or blaming the victim for making them angry.

Once the abuser releases the tension, a period of peace and compromise begins, when they use gifts, kindness, and loving gestures to bring a sense of calm to the relationship.

In turn, the victim has a release of healthy brain chemicals that make them feel better, bonding them to the abuser.

To maintain peace, the abuser justifies the abuse, assuring the victim that it will never happen again, making them believe that the worst is over. The cycle then repeats, with the victim never realizing that they are being manipulated and controlled.

The stable life that I had provided for Amanda, instead of bringing comfort, increased her anxiety. For most of her life, she had grown accustomed to the abuse cycle. The kinder I was, the higher her stress level became as she waited for the release of an incident so she could relax. The relaxation never came, though, making it impossible for her to unwind. It was truly tragic, for both of us.

In March of 2016, Amanda moved out. She became uncomfortable with the changes taking place around her and uncertain of how to deal with the love she was receiving. Her behavior created a distance between me and William and placed stress on the entire family. I was often forced to choose sides between my children and Amanda, and I did not like it. I had no means to cope with such changes, and no education or experience in dealing with abuse issues. I was doing the best I could, using my heart and my head, but it was not enough.

At the request of her stepmother, and with Amanda's consent, I brought her to her family. Inconsolable, I returned home and cried for weeks. Heartbroken, I blamed myself for having failed her, unable to comprehend that my love alone could not help her.

I sought solace from my husband, who offered a short hug and a lecture to *get over it*. The relationship meant nothing to him; it only mattered to me. I wanted a daughter and believed this was God's way of answering my prayer. I was wrong.

Damn my kind-hearted and loving nature! It always brought me grief.

Chapter 8

The Search Begins 1997

Twenty Years Earlier

I wanted to find my special someone, and in a hurry, because time was slipping through my fingers.

All my friends were married, and most were having children, and I desperately wanted to be a mother too. I believed that motherhood would remove the sense of loneliness I felt. Any children I had would love me for life, and this would eliminate my anxiety of being alone.

Though my career had begun to bloom, my love life was null and void. I had no marriage prospects, and I did not know where to start the journey for love. I had tried the bar scene, the school scene, and the work scene, but all avenues had left me empty handed.

By the time I was thirty, I was feeling desperate.

"How are you? You do not look yourself," my uncle asked when he was visiting one day. I was trying to hide my depression, but he saw through my façade; my downcast expression told the tale that my words did not.

As I began to cry, he glared at mom. "What is wrong with you? Can't you see how miserable she is?"

I wailed for what seemed like an eternity as he comforted me, patting my back. "There, there, darling. It will be okay." As I normally felt invisible, I loved him for noticing.

As much as I wanted a "special someone," I had no real sense of what a connection or relationship entailed. For most of my life, all I had known was the parent-child bond.

There were no men in my household, and there was no structure for me to use as a guide to define a normal, healthy relationship. I did not find it odd because I did not know any better.

I kept hoping that, someday, I would meet Mr. Right, and he would sweep me off my feet and take me away to a better life. I should have known better. Fairy tales do not belong in the real world.

Months later, I read an advertisement in the local newspaper for a new educational program offered in New Brunswick. Several of my friends had decided to attend, and they encouraged me to come along.

This was my chance to be able to study computer science, the path I had wanted to follow when I finished high school before my family interceded with their own plans.

Every ounce of me screamed to apply.

I wrote and passed their entrance exam, quit my job (much to the chagrin of my mother), and set out on my new adventure. My hope and enthusiasm renewed. I was filled with excitement and anticipation of what the future may have in store.

Mya and I had the finite details of the trip planned. She would accompany me to school, help set me up in my apartment, and then return home. It was only a twelve-month program, and I convinced her that time would fly by. On the day of our departure, I was scared and nervous, but nothing could have prepared me for the events that unfolded.

At the airport check-in, Mya had a panic attack. She began crying and could not catch her breath, overwhelmed with the thought of travelling alone on the return trip. It was too much for her to anticipate saying goodbye to me, so she refused to go.

With tears streaming down her face, she softly muttered, "I can't go, I just can't. I'm sorry." As they pulled Mya's luggage off the plane, we hugged and said our goodbyes.

My mind raced, uncertain how to manage the situation. The only answer forthcoming was to travel alone, since everything was packed, paid for, and on its way.

Upon arrival in New Brunswick, I rented a car and found a hotel to spend the night, and collect my composure. I was a wreck and in a strange place with strange people, but it was time for me to learn how to survive on my own.

My apartment was in a small building (only five floors), in the downtown district, and close to the ocean. The apartment was quaint, with a panoramic view of the water. It had secured access for safety, which gave me peace of mind. It was quiet and, most importantly to me, it was spotless.

It had a separate sitting room where I placed a bistro table and a tall, leafy, green plant. As I opened the doors, I inhaled the cool ocean breeze; the smell of salt air reminded me of home. I draped the windows with white lace curtains to provide a feeling of coziness and offer a sense of privacy.

The galley kitchen was fresh, with modern light oak cupboards and white appliances. The bathroom was clean, with a deep bathtub, soft pale-yellow walls, and beige floor tiles.

The walls in the main room were painted a neutral color, and there was one medium-sized window where I hung vertical blinds to block out the streetlights and conceal my bedroom from plain view. The new wall-to-wall gray carpet was comforting on the feet. I placed my floral pull-out couch opposite my waterbed in the center of the room, then my oak wooden coffee table, computer, and desk. I angled the dresser next to the bed to improve the aesthetics.

I was home.

It was my first time on my own. I loved that I could come and go as I pleased, and cook and eat what I wanted, when I wanted. I was in control, and I was happy. For the first time in my life, I felt free.

My time in technology school provided a two-fold opportunity – to study my selected subject matter, and to meet my potential future husband. Most of the men in school had girlfriends or significant others, but the world of online dating was a new, unfolding phenomenon.

I met folks from all over the world, playing games like checkers and backgammon in online games rooms.

The first gentleman that I connected with online was a Texan named Bob. He was older than me, had a daughter, and owned his own business. We chatted for three or four months.

I liked Bob's personality and the way he portrayed himself. He was smart, funny, good looking, and seemed sweet and sincere. We exchanged pictures and life stories. Our conversations were lively, and our banter was playful and friendly.

One day, just as I was leaving class, he called. As I answered, I heard, "Kate, I love you."

I thought I was dreaming! Stunned by his words, I told him I would return his call when I arrived home.

I was dialing his number as I entered the apartment. "Sorry, I was rushing to leave and didn't quite hear what you said."

He chuckled. "I said that I love you."

Uncertain how to respond, I wondered if it was possible to fall in love online. Having evaluated the probabilities, I decided that anything was possible. "I really like you too," I said, smiling.

He sent roses for my birthday, eleven red roses representing his love for me, and a single yellow rose to represent Texas. It deeply touched me.

I enjoyed spending time with him and developing our relationship, until the day he asked a horrible question.

"Is that really you in the picture?"

I laughed and responded sarcastically, "No." Then, giggling, replied, "Of course it's me, why do you ask?"

"Well, I do not like big girls, no offence, and I am not trying to be rude, but they do not turn me on. You look so beautiful and small in the photo, I just wanted to be sure."

"Oh, okay." My heart dropped to my boots.

I did not know how to tell him that I was larger than in the pictures we had exchanged. The one he had seen of me on the school web page was extremely flattering, I looked petite.

Once again, I was not enough. It was love – but with conditions. The connection was based on appearance, who I was as a person was irrelevant.

Feeling rejected, I knew it was only a matter of time before that relationship was over. Honestly, it ended with that one conversation.

Par for the course, I pulled away, retreated into my shell and safety zone, burying more pain in the depths of my soul. There was no point in surrendering my heart.

Slowly, I withdrew from the conversations, making excuses for my absence, and eventually ceasing all communication. Months passed before we spoke again, and I learned that he was bereft with my absence.

Emphatically declaring that his "I love you" had been sincere, he angrily questioned if I had any idea how long it took for him to get over me. He told me of the countless nights that he lay awake, wondering if I was okay or if something had happened to me.

I apologized, coldly stating that I did not think he really cared. After all, he was only interested in my size, not me. He was speechless.

In my mind, there was no point in continuing. You either love all of me or none of me, that is how I think. I have no time for conditional love, games, or lies.

Regardless of what I thought, wished, or wondered about our relationship, I had to move on.

Next, there was a guy from Oklahoma. We also chatted for a couple of months. He was a smooth talker, charming, handsome, and intelligent. He led me to believe that he was extremely interested in me, and there were no hang ups about weight as he also had a heavy frame. We discussed the possibility of a future together, and on the next long weekend, we met face to face.

The connection that had existed online faded away when we met in person. The friendly dialogue was replaced with deafening silence, and it made me extremely uncomfortable. Disenchanted, I came home early.

Within weeks, he was married, and once again, I felt deceived. I was nothing more than the untouched last dessert before his lifetime diet change.

I just did not get it. What was wrong with me?

No one asked me out. No one wanted to date me. Was I bad looking or have bad breath? Was I not fashionable? There must be something.

I was feeling lost and unloved as sadness, loneliness, and depression set in.

What I was searching for did not seem to exist, or my expectations were simply unreasonable. I did not think that a kind, educated, loving, tender, and affectionate man would be that difficult to find. It did not seem like a long, complicated list of characteristics and personality traits. The men in my family had those traits, how hard could it be?

What I did not realize at the time was that I wanted and needed much more than I had defined, and those qualities are as rare as the Hope Diamond.

Chapter 9

Mom's Illness – April 2016

In April of 2016, Mom became critically ill. She had spent her entire career in service to others, working long shifts, constantly walking on concrete floors around the hospital. At the end of her career, she developed health issues that rendered her incapable of doing many of the normal activities of her daily life. Lack of attention to her health caused her to suffer in pain every day.

One day, she fell in her living room and was unable to muster enough strength to get upright. She called for help, and the family arrived in droves – aunts, uncles, cousins, neighbors – each of us trying to find a way to get her up off the floor without success.

We called for paramedics who could bring the equipment needed to tend to her. After their assessment, it was determined that Mom would be admitted to hospital, as she was far more ill than we realized. The anti-inflammatory medication she was taking to cope with her pain had caused her kidneys to fail. The doctors told us that she had hours to live.

As she lay in her hospital bed, sleeping quietly, I gazed upon her sweet, plump, face. My thoughts transported me backwards to my youth and my relationship with my mother.

Mom always greeted life with a smile. She wanted me to be resilient, honest, generous, kind, and loving. She helped build my faith and my relationship with God, teaching me to pray regularly throughout my life, not only in times of crisis. Her values and beliefs heavily influenced every aspect of my life.

I love my mom and family, dearly. In many respects we are very alike, in others radically different.

Mom and I are both perfectionists, insisting on a clean and spotless home and everything done post haste. She was always demanding and impatient, often unreasonably so, and I grew to resent the control that I allowed her to have over me.

Growing up, the more she demanded, the more I felt like I could not meet her expectations – regardless of how hard I tried. We constantly butted heads, and the more educated I became, the more conflict arose. I tried to share alternate perspectives, but it was a waste of time as she would not listen or accept them. I was always wrong, in her eyes, even when there were times when I knew I was right.

Mom was so intransigent; there was simply no changing her. Her lack of flexibility frustrated me and made me feel unappreciated and undervalued.

Mya's relationship with Mom was different from mine, due in part to her medical condition. Mom was afraid to upset her out of fear that she would inflame her epilepsy, so Mya was given more leniency.

When the time came for us to obtain our driver's licenses, I had to wait until I was nineteen; Mya had a temper tantrum and received it one month after her eighteenth birthday.

At birthday parties, I would get cool presents, and Mya would cry until my grandmother bought her the same items the following day. I never asked for anything, I was simply happy to see her happy. Mya found it easy to say no to Mom. I never could; it was always *yes*.

The inconsistencies in treatment between me and Mya

increased routinely, with the excuse that she was not as strong. Tasks like cleaning the house or running errands fell to me.

Mya did not bake cakes or cookies or decorate the house for special occasions. She could sit and tell funny stories to make Mom and my friends laugh while I washed the windows, vacuumed the curtains, and painted the walls. Over time, I began to feel like Cinderella, but I always tried to make the best of it. I desperately wanted to make Mom proud, happy, and to bring her peace.

Although I had been groomed to accept that Mya was unable to do chores, I did not like it. The only person who ever seemed to notice the difference in the way our mother treated us was my uncle. Early on Saturday mornings, when he needed assistance to do something for Mom, he would pass by my door and head straight for Mya, getting her out of bed. It made me laugh heartily and she hated it. He did it so often, she eventually nicknamed me Queenie.

There were a host of insignificant incidents like these, which accumulated over time and contributed to the emotional void that grew within me. Each removed another piece of my confidence and security, confirming my irrational belief that I was different and not enough.

It is like saving pennies. A single penny seems worthless, but twenty years' worth of saving pennies could provide you with a fistful of dollars. My emotional bank account was in constant overdraft.

Mom pushed me to be the best, and I endeavored to rise to the occasion. I listened to her advice, dressed and spoke well, and engaged in activities that made me uncomfortable just to please her and make her proud. I did everything in my power to become the person she envisioned me to be.

As time passed, my disinterest in these events became evident, and I withdrew from center stage to my comfort zone. I suppose, in some respects, I did make her proud.

I do not think that my parents, especially Mom, ever realized the pressure they were putting on me to conform, to carry the load of expectations for both me and Mya. If that was not the case, it was truly how I felt, and it caused me grief, all the time. I was loved, and I realize that she was being protective of my sister, but putting parameters on a relationship that is supposed to be unconditional was daunting for me.

I do not know why, but after my parents separated, I felt a sense of obligation to Mom for having continuously put us first, and for sacrificing her happiness for ours. The feeling of indebtedness led me to make decisions to "repay" her for what she did for me and the sacrifices that she made.

I slogged three jobs to afford the books and supplies necessary to put myself through university, fulfilling her dream of me obtaining a degree. Mya, however, was offered to attend college or trade school because, according to Mom, the stress of university would be too great for her.

In many respects, I felt like I had failed Mom by never reaching the standards she had set for me, or the ones I had set for myself. Having constantly been compared to the girls I had gone to school with, the honors class, I realized that I was not successful like my classmates, most of whom had blossoming careers.

At twenty-nine, I had a job, but not a career; I was no longer a virgin, and there were no prospects for marriage. By Mom's standards, the future did not look bright.

Shaped by her influence, I had become a people pleaser and forgotten that I also needed to please myself.

A heavy sigh escaped my lips as my thoughts returned to the hospital room. As I watched her sleeping, a sense of sadness came over me, and I hung my head, filled with regret.

I wished that she had taught me to be stronger, to stand up for my beliefs, and to defend myself; to allow me to fail and view it as an opportunity to try again, instead of feeling incompetent. I wished she had allowed me to have normal relationships, like everyone else, instead of sheltering us; to have had the opportunity to meet diverse classes of people, and to meet great people so I could emulate them.

At fifty, faced with the reality that my life may never improve, a sense of desperation swept over me as I realized how many dreams have been left unfulfilled. Mom's life was almost over, mine was more than half spent; maybe it was time I tried to find happiness before it was too late.

Mya shifted restlessly in her chair, exploring my facial expressions, uncertain of my thoughts. Her fingers tapping on her blue leather purse, waiting impatiently for news.

As the physician returned, to advise of mom's prognosis, I sat upright, glancing fearfully at Mya. We were not prepared for anything other than her survival. We could not bear to lose her; she was our rock and solace, regardless of our individual perspectives.

The doctor advised that, with a variety of medications and fluids, her body had begun to respond. She was not out of the woods, but she was improving slowly and consistently. A month later, she came home.

Unable to perform any household tasks, prepare meals, or bathe and care for herself, we arranged home care. Grateful for her survival, and optimistic she would be present for more years of my life, I offered a prayer of thanksgiving.

As I tried to catch my breath, the speed of my life seemed to go into overdrive and, a week later, I was gasping for air when James was paralyzed.

The lesson to be learned this year was going to be a big one, because the universe was being cold and heartless, shaking me to my core.

Chapter 10

Meeting Liam

Twenty Years Earlier
As my search for someone special continued, I met Liam. Living in different provinces, we met online and chatted about a variety of topics – family, friends, education, line of work – the usual getting to know each other questions.

He was smart, attentive, romantic, and had a dry sense of humor, which I loved.

We shared pictures, and at first glance, I thought he was an average-looking guy with a nice smile. I sent my graduation picture, which I thought was stunning. My hair and makeup were flawless, my teeth were perfectly white. I looked like a professional model.

He was the baby of the family, with three older brothers and three older sisters. He was younger than me, loved music, and could sing. He was kind, and based on our conversations, I knew that he treated his family well, especially his mom, nieces, and nephews.

He was an animal lover who rescued dogs and nurtured them back to health. Like me, he enjoyed being social, having fun, and participating in community activities.

Based on his story telling, he made it obvious that family was a high priority in his life. This was an important characteristic to me because I wanted a strong father figure for any potential children. I needed a man who wanted to put his family first and keep his family together.

When he shared pictures and stories of a vacation he had taken with his family, I sensed how much they meant to him, and it touched me – love of, and loyalty to, family are character traits I value highly. Overall, he seemed like a great guy. He had potential and, in my eyes, was a diamond in need of polishing.

After many weeks of talking online and by phone, we decided to meet in person and spend a week together. I chose a bar downtown near my apartment for our initial meeting, a public location for my safety, or in case I wanted to exit quickly. A couple of my friends from school were there for support, to give their nod of approval or their head shake of rejection.

As he entered, I sized him up from top to bottom. He was the opposite of the men I was ordinarily attracted to. He was muscular, rugged-looking and very masculine – a stark contrast to the gentle baby-faced men who typically appealed to me.

Dressed in jeans and a plaid shirt, he was clean shaven, tall, slim, and his brown hair was styled in a short, military haircut. His teeth were perfect, and his smile was beautiful.

I waved to get his attention, and as he walked toward me, he extended his hand for a handshake, introducing himself.

Initially awkward, we quickly became comfortable with one another, chatting just as we had online. We shared a couple of drinks, and I introduced him to my friends, who liked his modest nature.

Hours later, we left the bar to get a bite to eat. Any anxiety that I had felt earlier had dispersed, replaced with attraction and inquisitiveness.

As the night ended, we retreated to the apartment and chatted for the rest of the evening. Sometime before dawn, we drifted off to sleep; he on my pull-out sofa bed, me in my waterbed.

In the morning, I made bacon and eggs for breakfast, showered, and headed to school.

When I returned to the apartment, I discovered him rooting through my belongings. I requested an explanation and he responded, innocently, that he had only been looking for a towel. I was uncomfortable with him rifling through my personal effects. I did not like him being nosy; it meant that he was not trustworthy, and I had always been too trusting.

While I waited for him to dress, I went online to do schoolwork and discovered that he had also accessed my computer files. I could only assume that he had been checking to see who else I was chatting with online, and there were several people. It raised a flag of concern, but I ignored it, wanting to give him the benefit of the doubt.

The sun was shining as we left my apartment, rented a car, and drove along the coast. We watched in awe as surfers struggled to paddle out to the open water, the white crests intense, hoping to catch the next wave, despite the freezing cold temperatures. We dined in chic bohemian restaurants, shopped at the local malls, walked in the national park, and visited historic sites.

I brought him to my school and introduced him to more of my friends. He was responsive to the women and engaged with them in casual conversation but shied away from talking to the guys. I found it odd that he did not react the same to all my friends.

Growing up, Mom frequently commented that the best way to a man's heart was through his stomach. Later in the week, I cooked a delicious turkey dinner with chocolate cake and lemon pie for dessert, and I invited three couples from school to join us.

At the end of the evening, after everyone had left, Liam kissed me, and my lips melded to his. He completely caught me off guard, and fireworks exploded in my mind.

Wow, he sure could kiss! Slowly, his hands began exploring my body and I gave him access. We moved to my bed and made love, falling asleep in each other's arms.

The next morning, he told me that he was falling in love with me and asked if I would move in with him after my graduation. Thoughts of the past few days swirled in my brain. We were compatible and I did enjoy his company and conversation. There was no denying that I was falling for him, even if there were aspects of his behavior that made me hesitant and uncertain.

I weighed his request against the thoughts of returning home. Graduation was four weeks away and I had no plan in place. I hated the thought of returning home without a job, having to listen to Mom tell me what a waste of time and money this experience had been, knowing that I would once again lose my freedom. I could not face it.

I jumped at the chance of going somewhere new and starting a new life, even if it was with a man I barely knew. I was willing to take the risk and dove headfirst into my new adventure.

I smiled, "Sure. I will move in with you."

The rest of the week passed quickly, and Liam prepared to return home to his life and responsibilities. I walked him to the bus terminal, and we kissed goodbye. I waited anxiously, hoping he would turn around to wave goodbye again, but he never did.

Instead, he called as soon as he had settled in on the bus and at every subsequent stop on the return trip. Many times, during those calls, he debated getting off the bus and turning around, because he did not want to leave me. I smiled, confident that the future was looking bright and positive. In a few weeks, we would be together again.

I looked for work in Liam's hometown and found a job as a management consultant for a popular technology company.

Liam arrived on the evening of graduation with his pickup truck to collect me and my belongings and bring us to our new home. He was a little worried when he realized the amount of furniture I wanted to take from my apartment, and he forced me to ship some items to Mom. His truck was not designed for moving an entire apartment, and he made that abundantly clear.

I had recently purchased a beautiful brown leather coat and handed it to him, requesting that he place it on the front seat. I had filled the pockets with the last of my cash, so we could purchase snacks along the way, as well as my winter gloves to keep my hands warm, because it was bitterly cold.

As we drove through the provinces, I saw something fly into the air from the back of the truck. I screamed at him, "Stop! Stop the truck! That was my coat!" He muttered that there was nowhere to pull over and kept driving.

I did not want to make a scene, but I was furious. I loved that coat! Oh well, if there was nowhere to stop then there was little I could do. I leaned my head against the window and drifted off to sleep. I wondered what to expect, where I was going, and if I had made the right decision.

When we reached our destination, he drove me around his town, up one street and down another. "What do you think?" he asked.

"Well, show me the rest and I'll let you know."

"This is it."

Grimacing, I stared at him in disbelief, thinking to myself, *Where have you taken me*?

I was a city girl dropped in the middle of nowhere. Open

fields of corn, soy, wheat, and acres of undeveloped land stretched as far as the eye could see. I did not know what to think, and I wondered how I would adjust to this unfamiliar environment and new relationship.

Everything was happening so fast. A new life meant changes, and I had to keep an open mind and learn to adapt. I decided to be resilient and try to make it work. I was too tired to care, it was late, and I wanted to sleep. I would see the rest in the light of a new day.

When I woke and surveyed my surroundings, I cringed. I hated the apartment. The cupboards were a chestnut brown from the 1970s; the walls were a dingy beige, crying out for a fresh coat of paint; the carpet was dirty, stained, and needed replacing. The bathroom was clean, but the baby blue tile from a different era let me know that this was not like home. It was far below the standards to which I had been accustomed.

The apartment was undecorated and did not feel cozy; the furniture was scarce. There were no pictures or artwork on the walls; an old metal table stood alone in the tiny kitchen; the couch was covered in grease stains; double-tiered end tables with skinny legs protruded into the living room, where a motorcycle was propped against the wall. The bedroom had white walls with blue feather painting, attempting to appear modern. Thank goodness I had taken my own furniture with me.

Appalled to see his clothes strewn all over the bedroom floor, I immediately began tidying up, looking for a place to store them. He apologized, indicating that he had just moved in and had not had the time to get things sorted. I was such a neat freak. The first stop was to buy a dresser for our belongings.

I was shocked when I learned that he had obtained this apartment as a step up for me, compared to where he was previously living.

I had to remind myself that I could not penalize a person because they have no money. Work with what you have been given, be creative.

There was one corner store, a butcher shop, a couple of garages, a Walmart, a Canadian Tire, and a bank in town. It was isolated and remote. There were few places to work and limited options for entertainment.

As we drove around, I was taken aback. There was no Tim Horton's, McDonald's, take outs restaurants, or diners, and no drug store. Any of those essential locations were an hour away in either direction. This was going to be an adjustment! Shopping and dining in my normal world were located within a fifteen-minute radius.

My life had radically changed overnight. Everything would be okay, *wouldn't it?*

Chapter 11

The Hospital Admission – 2016

They brought James to his room and moved him into a new bed. Initially, we were in a wing of the hospital by ourselves as they determined the cause of the paralysis. Believing it could have been viral, they isolated us from other patients to prevent any potential spread. His room was small, and there did not seem to be any room for us to stay with him. I began to fret.

Once the blood work reported normal, they moved us to a much larger room with two beds, a private bath, and a panoramic view of the hills outside the hospital. The new bed converted from a bed to a chair in the event James wanted to change positions and sit up for a while. It intrigued me that there were such simple advances in medical equipment.

Nurses appeared with bags of medication, blood pressure equipment, thermometers, and a host of other devices to monitor his condition. They established an IV line, and the steroids began flowing into his body.

I did not know what to expect, hoping that after one bag he would miraculously be normal again; but normal did not arrive that day, or the next.

The doctors performed more tests, including a spinal tap to examine the fluid in the brain and spine, blood work to look for anomalies, and another CT scan.

As the days passed, my stress and disappointment grew. I

repeatedly assured James that he had to be patient. "God works in mysterious ways darling, have faith." He was such an amazing child, he trusted every word I spoke, believing normal would return… eventually.

I would not let anyone speak negatively to or around him. I stayed positive, and insisted all visitors were positive as well.

At the end of the week, new physicians arrived on the unit to study and examine him. Transverse Myelitis was such a rare condition, doctors from every discipline were coming to investigate the extraordinary case. James was examined and assessed, until finally, we had progress.

As they conducted the neurological tests to determine his levels of sensation and touch, he twitched his big toe. I gasped and held my breath as the doctor asked him to move it again. By the third time, we were screaming and dancing, as we realized he was moving it voluntarily! It was the first positive sign we had had in a week.

I kissed and hugged him, as he giggled and laughed, excited with his progress. I must have asked him to move it at least fifty times that evening, every time repeating, "God won't fail us, James, He is a kind and loving God!"

As night fell, I slept in the bed next to his, with my rosary beads in my hands, praying for hours at a time, often falling asleep in the middle of prayer.

When morning arrived, I bathed him, ensured he ate breakfast, and then left to go home, get my own shower, and head to work.

I asked my boss if he had any issue with me working out of James' room because I was far too distracted to remain in the office. I could have virtual meetings by video conference, and it should not impact my performance. He declined, saying that other managers had similar issues, and he could not treat me differently.

I was shocked, angry, and deeply hurt by his response. My previous supervisors were very flexible and accommodating in extenuating circumstances, and I could not understand his refusal. I went to the vice president, who granted me permission and sent an IT team to the nursing unit to make the necessary arrangements for me to have access in James' room.

As news of his condition spread, our friends and family brought gifts, teachers gave him homework, and clergy arrived to pray with us.

What I had hoped was going to be an admission for a couple of days went on far longer than I could have ever imagined. Days turned into weeks turned into three and a half months.

James' room became a gathering place for staff, friends, family, teachers, nurses, and doctors; for meetings, schooling, medicine, card games, and meals. I never left his side and I never stopped praying.

Liam returned to work and offered to take turns spending the night with James, but I would not hear of it. The occasions that he did stay, he requested advice on how to assist him, where items were located, and called me, disturbing my sleep, and defeating his purpose in being there. I suggested that he stay home, care for William and the dog, and run the house; he agreed.

During the second week of James' hospitalization, my cousin died in a car accident. I watched from James' room as they held a memorial service for her. As I watched, I felt sad for her friends and family; but, as selfish as it sounds, I was grateful that it was not James.

The staff from my department, and other departments I had previously managed, were incredibly kind to me and my family.

They brought wine, baskets of toys, candy, games, and books, overwhelming me with their compassion, generosity, and empathy. It felt like Christmas.

As I rummaged through the contents of the colorful baskets, my memories carried me away, fast as a rushing current, to previous Christmases.

Mya and I attended an all-female Catholic school where the principles of sacrifice and community were embedded in our being, as well as the values of integrity, compassion, sensitivity, and serving others. The education provided a solid, spiritual foundation, which was encouraged and strengthened by Mom and her family.

When Mya and I were children, Mom made Christmas an unforgettable experience, surprising us with jewelry, new clothes, and perfume. The house looked festive, as Christmas decorations – Santa, reindeers, angels, poinsettias, and homemade crocheted ornaments – appeared in every nook and cranny. The scent of cinnamon, cloves, and all spice from homemade cakes and cookies wafted into every room and greeted visitors at the front door.

Mya and I were taught to be kind. We loved to give to the less fortunate and those in need, it was a trait bred into us by our family. Every Christmas, we called the Salvation Army, requesting a family in need of assistance that we could help, people with good hearts who were struggling.

I recall one time when we were provided the name of a single dad who was delivering hampers to the poor. We collected money, food, clothes, toys, and donations, and brought it to his home in time for Christmas. Granted access by the property owner, Mya and I filled the empty fridge and placed the presents under the tree.

After Christmas, the family reached out to us to express their gratitude, proclaiming it one of the best Christmases that they had ever experienced. I will never forget that moment, the joy I felt and the happiness that filled me. I enjoyed being charitable because it is genuine giving, expecting nothing in return, and it inspired me to do more.

Mya and I did these acts for many people over the years because we sincerely love to give. I wish I could have been a philanthropist. I suppose, on a much smaller scale, I am.

Unannounced, the floodgates of memories opened swiftly, shifting to a previous Christmas with Liam, erasing the genuine smile that had temporarily spread across my face.

I loved Christmas. For me, it was truly the most wonderful, magical time of the year. I loved to shop, give gifts, and surprise others to make them feel loved, expressing how special they were to me.

Naturally, given my upbringing, I wanted the same thing for my children, but this particular year, there was no extra money to buy gifts once the bills were paid.

Our financial struggles had increased once the children had arrived. There had not been enough time to build a financial safety net and it was a huge problem. I used my savings to keep us afloat, but it was futile, and the debt began to sink us.

Though I tried to move ahead, it felt like we took two steps forward and one step back. In mid-November, I called Mom, panicking, asking for her assistance with Christmas. Despite her limited income, she purchased a ton of presents for the kids. As they arrived in dribs and drabs a couple of weeks before Christmas, I had one less thing to worry about. I relaxed, and the stress level dropped. With the boys' presents out of the way, I managed to save a few dollars to purchase small personal items for Liam, and I assumed he would get something small for me to put under the tree.

On Christmas morning, William opened his presents, filled with excitement. He called his grandmother to thank her for the gifts and wrote a thank you letter to Santa. James, still a baby, did not understand the concept of Christmas and was happy with his bottle of milk. Liam curiously opened his gifts, and I sat quietly, waiting for it to be my turn.

I cleaned up the wrapping paper and organized the gifts under the tree, believing that my gifts were hidden until a later time. Liam had surprised me late in the night on other occasions, and I assumed this would be the same.

I sat on the couch watching television as the hours passed. "I know we didn't have much money, but didn't you get me anything? A card? Chocolates? Something?"

Unable to look me in the eye, he hung his head sheepishly. "No. Nothing."

I stared at him in disbelief, "Nothing?"

"No," he whispered.

Deeply hurt, I disappeared to our bedroom to cry. It was the first time in my life that I had never gotten a present; nothing, not even a card.

Later in the day, Mom and Mya called to wish me a Merry Christmas and asked about the gifts I had received. I lied, as I choked back tears, swallowing the lump that had formed in my throat. "I had new nighties, and some new clothes, nothing too extravagant."

Mya then proceeded to tell me all the beautiful gifts her husband had given her, and Mom listed the lovely presents she had bought, just as they did every year. I was happy for them, but, inside, a part of me died. The little girl who had loved Christmas with all her heart suddenly hated the most wonderful time of the year.

All I could think was, *how could he*? He could have put aside enough money for a card or a cheap box of chocolates, something to show me that he loved me.

It was the first and last time I ever let that happen. Every Christmas from then on, whether he had purchased gifts or not, I would buy something for myself to have under the tree, so the children could see me open something.

Back in James' hospital room, I stared at the caramel plush teddy bear that had triggered my recollections, and a tear rolled slowly down my cheek. I quickly brushed it away with the memory.

Focus on the positive and be grateful for what you have, you cannot change the past, you can only move forward.

Chapter 12

The Engagement, Honeymoon, and Marriage

I met his friends and family and we settled into our new life. It was different from the life I had known; these people were farmers, early risers, and knew nothing about the hospital environment that I had grown to love.

I was unable to contribute to their conversations as they discussed machinery, manufacturing, and harvesting. My social interactions dwindled to two couples, instead of the tens of people with whom I was familiar at home. I was out of my element, and a sense of isolation settled into my bones, something that I had not previously experienced.

Every couple needs friends, people with different occupations and from different social classes, to provide alternate perspectives. It keeps the mind open and helps to set a base line for what a normal relationship should look like. Our limited interactions with others led me to rely heavily on Liam as my source of conversation, strength, and comfort. In doing so, the seeds of an unhealthy foundation were laid, though I believed we were a normal, intimate couple. I depended on him for everything.

During the early months of our relationship, Liam was attentive and loving. He would frequently leave me love notes in my lunch bag to make me smile, on special occasions he would even write touching poetry; he loved to cook my favorite meals and surprise me with gifts; and, although he had limited financial resources, he always found a way to bring me flowers. I loved to have our home filled with their scents and colors.

We shared the responsibilities of a home, and spent a lot of time together, with family and friends. Our relationship was intimate and sexually charged. I felt loved beyond measure.

On his way home from work one day, a few months after the move, Liam presented me with a bouquet of wildflowers. He stated that they reminded him of me: sweet, wild, strong, and beautiful.

He was deeply in love with me; his words and actions communicated his love for me through the most beautiful ways. He frequently compared my personality and demeanor to Lady Diana Spencer (Princess Diana) and Mother Theresa. He wooed me with romance and sweet gestures, and I folded like a house of cards.

One evening, in the spring, he bent down on one knee in our living room, his eyes like sparkling stars, "Kate, I love you. You are the most amazing woman I have ever met. I promise, if you give me a chance, I will do everything in my power to make you happy and give you a good life. It would be my honor to have you as my wife. Will you marry me?"

I stared at the half-carat diamond ring in his hand and wondered how he could afford such an elaborate piece of jewelry.

My eyes searched his smiling face as I debated my response. He made me feel loved and desired; we were both getting older; we both wanted a family; I was already thirty-one.

Tick, tock. Tick, tock. Tick, tock. The sound of my pounding biological clock. *Tick, tock.*

Caught up in the moment and the exciting possibility of being a bride, I smiled widely. "Yes, I will marry you," I replied.

We hugged, kissed, and called our families to share the good news. Our families were happy for us, but shocked with the speed of the relationship.

As exciting as it was, I was not really interested in the engagement. My priority was to become a mother before I was too old to have children, and within a few months, I became pregnant.

When I told Liam, he jumped up and down and then lay on the floor of the living room, repeatedly saying, "I am going to be a dad! We are having a baby! Woohoo!"

Mom cried, devastated that I was pregnant before I was married.

I was in no rush to walk down the aisle, but I did want the stability of a fiancé and a father for my child. I was excited about becoming a mother, but nervous about becoming a wife.

There were inconsistencies in his behavior that made me uncomfortable, and I needed reassurance before making a commitment. In the worst-case scenario, I would raise the baby by myself; in the best, I would be a mother and have the happy family that I desperately craved.

He was a drinker and a smoker. I grew up in a house of women who had never had a glass of champagne, let alone any beer or hard alcohol. I never had a gauge of how much was too much.

Well, no one is perfect, certainly not me. He could have had worse characteristics.

"Wait to be married" was my gut instinct.

"You can't bring a bastard into the world!" Mom cried, ashamedly, doling out the guilt by the bucket-load. She was not pleased that her devoutly religious daughter was having a baby out of wedlock.

The day of our wedding was cloudy and overcast. I was sick with laryngitis and had a temperature of 102 degrees Fahrenheit. I was so clammy that the makeup would not stay on my face, and I needed a lozenge to recite my vows. In hindsight, I guess those were signs from the universe not to get married.

My parents walked me down the aisle of our local church and gave me away to the man they believed would love me and care for me for the rest of my life. Liam gazed into my eyes, held my hand, and rubbed my arm tenderly for most of the ceremony.

Our reception was in the dining room of a posh high-end hotel, and since Mom had paid for the catering and the decorations, she decided on the guest list.

Being pregnant and ill was not a good combination for the night of the wedding. I disappeared to our room on multiple occasions to rest, but Mom led a search party to locate me, insisting that I dance with the wedding party.

I really did not feel up for it, but she lectured. "This is one of the biggest nights in your life. The guests are waiting. Get down there, dance, and have a fun time."

I groaned. "Sure, Mom."

I put on a smile and danced as she requested.

The remainder of the night I spent roaming around, speaking to guests, and being a good hostess. I could not wait for midnight to come so I could go to bed. When midnight finally arrived, I all but ran up to our room where Liam and I consummated the marriage and promptly fell asleep.

The honeymoon phase of our marriage was happy, carefree, romantic, and filled with laughter. We had so much to learn about each other and enjoyed spending every available second exploring our needs and wants, building our relationship. We moved out of the apartment, built a new home in his quiet town, and prepared for parenthood.

Like any newly married couple, we went everywhere together; to the grocery store, the malls in the neighboring city, visiting Liam's friends and family. We went fishing, camping, touring, and out to dinner; we attended community events, dances, and parties. We drove across the border on weekends to several states in the USA for dinner, and when money or air miles points allowed, travelled from our new home to my previous home to see my family.

Never bored, there was always something to do, somewhere to go, and something to see. We visited the neighboring cities frequently and toured the numerous historic sites, including the war and science museums. We searched for quaint restaurants with my favorite foods – Chinese and Italian – and ate there frequently. One restaurant owner enjoyed our patronage and always had "our table" ready.

To most, it was obvious that we were in love. Outwardly, we were a very respectful, affectionate, happy couple, holding hands, kissing frequently, and look at each other lovingly. We would share our meal and desserts with each other, chat about current events, and dream about the future.

Shortly after getting married, I was laid off from my technology position, and I was rattled, as I had never before been out of work. Panicking, I accepted the first job that presented itself, a clerk at the bank in his small community. While it was not ideal, it helped pay the bills.

The pay at the bank was less than half of what I had been making, I had student debt for the first time in my life from technical school, and credit card payments to make. My pay was no longer enough to cover it all.

Liam told me to be calm, it would work out. I trusted and believed him. He was wrong, I was wrong. Things got worse.

Several months into our marriage, the pressure began to mount, and Liam began inciting arguments about old boyfriends, finances, and the cost of bringing a baby into the world. I focused on the issue at hand, which was how we were going to manage financially with a new baby, but Liam began lashing out, and insulting me.

I quickly learned that he had anger issues, and it made me extremely uneasy. I would try to alleviate the stress by changing the subject or injecting a little humor.

Bob had called to check on me, to see how life was going in my new town and with my new relationship. I thought it was considerate and sweet of him to call. I try not to burn my bridges; you never know when you will need someone's assistance or guidance in your life. Liam never understood that concept; his mindset was that men and women cannot be friends because men want sex – period.

As we hurled hateful words at each other after the call, I told him that I was friends with Bob, and I wanted to remain friends with him. There was no harm, and certainly no ill intentions on my end. I was a married woman, and I had every intention of staying faithful and loyal to the relationship that I had sought for so long. I constantly reassured Liam of my faithfulness and love for him, but he refused to accept or believe me.

True to form, Liam believed that I was only interested in sex. I was highly offended. I was far from the loose woman that he was portraying me to be.

As the argument continued, I was shocked when he had the audacity to ask if our baby, formed in love, was his child. I was completely taken aback and stunned as I stared at him, bewildered with the accusation.

I was the closest thing to a virgin that a thirty-one-year-old woman in my generation could be. His insults had the same impact as being punched in the face—unexpected and excruciating.

Uncertain how to respond, I stood silently unable to speak with the words he just hurled at me, though he was acutely aware of the pain he was causing me.

Frustrated with his behavior and cruel words, the tears flowed, the anger overwhelming me, the pain fresh and bleeding. Such an accusation did not deserve a response. I ran to the bedroom sobbing; my spirit obliterated for the first time in our marriage.

Although I did not know it at the time, his jealous behavior was his first attempt to control me, and the first block that he erected on the wall that he began building between us. Fearful of intimacy, his self-sabotaging thinking was the second.

Doubtful of having a successful relationship, he kept pushing me away instead of pulling me closer, believing that I was too good for him.

Chapter 13

Healing – 2016

As the days passed, James' body began responding more consistently, and his feet and legs regained partial sensation and movement. Gradually, he learned to move from his bed to a wheelchair using a transfer board. This gave him the freedom to leave his room and play basketball in his wheelchair with his brother and friends. It offered him encouragement, and a way to maintain a positive outlook. About two weeks into his hospitalization, we met his physiotherapist, Susie.

Susie celebrated every win with James and offered hope at every turn. Heaven-sent, she oozed positivity and taught him to embrace his condition. She showed him how to live a full and happy life. She was optimistic, a source of strength and encouragement, and James loved her.

She pushed him out of his comfort zone, encouraged him when he did not want to go on, and did everything humanly possible to help him regain his ability to walk. He had physiotherapy every day for months, and despite the constant challenges, there was considerable progress.

My birthday gift that year was to watch my son walk again. I choked back sobs of joy and relief as he took steps toward me using his customized walker. The emotion that I felt while watching him overcome his struggles was indescribable. It was the best gift that I have ever received, and I felt blessed.

It is extraordinarily difficult to watch your teenager try to regain a modicum of normalcy. I recall receiving one very difficult report from the physicians; James sobbed uncontrollably when he heard it. It was the only time he broke down during his time in hospital, and one of the first times he had cried since he was a baby. He had been strong, resilient, and persistent throughout the whole ordeal, but knowing that there was a high likelihood that some of his sensation would never return crushed his spirit. I implored the doctors for other options, but there were none.

I rocked him gently in my arms and tried to reassure him. "You aren't alone, my love, we will get through this together."

I poured all my energy into healing and assisting him – every day, four times a day, for the next three years – constantly praying for change.

We followed the same routine every day. I would get him up and ready for school; pick him up at lunch and bring him home; drive back to school; pick him up after school; and bring him home at the end of the day. There were medical procedures to perform in each instance. It was mentally and physically exhausting for both of us. I cried when the function never returned in his legs, disillusioned with God and bitter because He did not heal him.

Innately stubborn, I refused to give up and maintained a cheerful outlook, no matter what fate threw at me.

As time passed, I feared for his psychological health. I was concerned with how he would cope with walking abnormally, and I prepared him for people staring at him as much as I could. I frequently reminded him, "When you find someone staring at you, watching you walk, or looking at your brace, smile at them. They do not mean to stare; they are curious about your condition and in awe at your strength and coping mechanisms."

It may not have been the best advice, but I did not think it was the worst either. I also told him , if people ask questions, to educate them about his condition, as you never know who your story could impact.

The feeling of being uncomfortable and different was not new to me. I had plenty of stories to share with him that would convey those emotions; experiences from my childhood that I carried with me throughout my life. I began rambling about my past, relaying the funny stories, and offering encouragement.

As a child, I had had to wear hideous corrective boots to bed – they had looked like shoes with the toes cut out of them and a bar between them – because my feet turned slightly inward. When I ran, I would trip and fall, injuring my legs, leaving the skin black and blue. Wearing the boots made me very conscious of the way I walked and looked. I eventually became so paranoid about my feet and gait that I thought about and corrected every step before I took it, until finally, it became automatic.

I enjoyed being a wallflower, sitting quietly in the background observing those around me, but embarrassment became second nature.

My introduction to menstruation had been at the age of thirteen, while at a family picnic. My mother, unabashedly, sang out across the countryside, "Does anyone have a pad? Kate started her period." Cringing, I could feel the blood rush to my face as it turned cherry red. I prayed for the ground to open and swallow me whole, but my prayers went unanswered.

Then there is the matter of hair growth. All young women grow hair under their arms, but most have mothers sensible enough to teach them to shave before they look like a gorilla. Not mine.

I was not enlightened until the gentleman who owned the pharmacy on the corner pulled me aside and said, "Please go home and ask your mother to teach you how to shave."

I had so much hair growth that it looked like large black bushes protruding from my armpits, clearly visible when my arms hung normally by my side. Monkeys had nothing on me!

As I shared my stories, we giggled and laughed, and I reminded him that if I could survive, he could too. He smiled deeply, contented with my funny stories, and filled with renewed optimism.

In times of despair, God sends an angel or two to offer support and encouragement.

There was a doctor that I had had a crush on and whom I dearly adored. When I was a junior employee, he would stop in for a visit on Friday evenings, after his medical rounds, to say *hi* and have a chat before leaving for the day. He was tall, lean, and handsome, with a distinctive Australian accent. He was a huge flirt with blue eyes and a devilish grin. He would frequently make me blush and stammer, and still does to this day.

One day, not long after James' diagnosis, he must have sensed how troubled I was, and opened his arms for a hug. Little did he know how badly I had needed a hug that day. We have been doing "hug therapy" ever since.

Those hugs provided the strength that I needed to keep going and lessened the feelings of extreme loneliness I was experiencing. There were days when those hugs were the only thing to keep me going. He may never know how much I appreciated them or how much they brightened my day. His simple act of kindness offered faith that people cared.

My coworkers who supported me through James' trials were

understanding and encouraging. They kept the department running by attending meetings and ensuring the completion of daily tasks. I have no words to express my profound gratitude to them for their acts of kindness; they lifted me up when I thought I was drowning, and when there was no oxygen left, they breathed life into me.

As a mother, all I can say is that a piece of you dies with the abilities that don't return: the inability to run, jump, play football with his friends, or walk normally. Simple activities will now be an ordeal, potentially for the rest of his life.

It leads to questions that never previously came to mind. Like, will he ever be able to have children? In my mind, I questioned whether he would find a girl who he could someday make his wife. I repeatedly assured him that he would meet someone who would love him when the time was right, and like all things in life, he had to be patient.

Thankful for the moments of positivity, I mustered the energy to keep going, but fate was cruel and heartless, and the relentless attacks on my sanity continued.

In August of that year, I lost the executive administrator position to Edward, one of my colleagues, and it crushed me.

I had spent my entire career working toward the goal of being administrator, putting in long hours, volunteering for additional work, and educating myself in preparation for the role.

Edward and I met when a management position became vacant in our department. He approached me, asking if I would speak to my boss and put in a good word for him. I liked Edward, he was fun and positive, intelligent and, I believed, a good fit for our department. I convinced my boss to hire someone who could speak to the challenges of the department on a clinical level, and he agreed. Edward successfully obtained position.

Believing he was my friend, I took him under my wing and attempted to teach him everything I knew, but he did not appear interested once he had gotten the role. I quickly learned that he wanted a flexible position because of his children and their extra-curricular activities.

I understood the challenges of life with a family, but he spent more time out of the office than in it, which frustrated me. Gary, our boss, would call looking for Edward and I would excuse his absence saying, "Oh, he must be in a meeting, I'll have him call you." Then I would call around looking for him, often finding him at home.

I covered for Edward because I was the person who had spoken to his work ethic and ability to perform effectively, and I did not want to be embarrassed. To keep things flowing smoothly in the department and not raise suspicion, I prepared the reports that our boss requested. Some days, he was not in the office for more than four hours a day, while I worked ten to twelve hours. I did not mind doing the work because he was my friend, and I believed that he would return the favor at some point.

When Gary retired, I submitted my application for his position, confident that I was a contender. Gary and I had spent time together handing off files, discussing the status of various projects, and teaching me how to perform the duties of administrator. Based on his behavior, I thought I all but had the position.

I waited patiently, but I did not receive a call for an interview, and I found it very odd. Days later, I was in a meeting and was caught off guard when Edward arrived. I tried to maintain my composure as we discussed the interview questions and his responses, but in the back of my mind I was angry, especially when he casually claimed that he had used examples of my work as his own.

My blood boiled! I was furious because I had not been interviewed, and internally irate because he had been and had used examples of my work. How dare he!

I stewed for several days and finally mustered the courage to call the vice president. "Why wasn't I interviewed?" I asked her.

"Sorry. It was an oversight. Please come in."

I did not believe her, since it was my observation that politics and social cliques played a prevalent role in position assignment within the organization. They had had no intention of bringing me in, it was a pity interview to keep me quiet.

Truthfully, I was in no state of mind for a job interview, given the events that had transpired that year. Instead of being calm and focusing on my accomplishments during the interview, I was angry and argumentative.

Internally, I was having a meltdown, suffering from lack of sleep, physical and mental exhaustion, and sheer frustration. I spent my time focusing on the fact that it was my work and not Edward's, rather than on my accomplishments and what my years of experience would bring to the position. As I walked away, I knew I had no chance of being successful, though I prayed to God I would be.

The announcement of Edward's success in obtaining the position came a week later. I was utterly devastated, but I had no one to blame but myself.

The first three actions he took as administrator were to reduce my work, cut my pay, and move my office. This was my friend, the person I had gone to bat for with my boss.

Edward denied my every request for assistance, regardless of the simplicity.

During one of the most challenging times in my life, he offered no support, sympathy, or empathy. His behavior stunned me.

Instead of being a friend, he was making a statement as my new boss, clearly indicating that the friendship had meant nothing to him. I was gutted.

Work was my strength, my source of confidence and comfort, and now it was stripped from my hands. The rock-solid foundation that I had built my life on was slowly disappearing, and I stood by helplessly, watching it crumble to the ground.

My qualifications and accomplishments had meant nothing. All the work that I had done, the changes I had made, and the long hours I had put in were meaningless. It was all about appearances and social circles.

The storm kept twisting, savagely sucking the life from my body and spirit, discontent until I was on my knees and pleading for mercy.

In September, we had a flood in the basement of our new home and, although it was a minor inconvenience, it added to the troubles that were mounting by the day.

James was discharged from the hospital a few weeks later, and we were faced with accessibility issues, which were completely foreign to us. Ramps were installed to bring James into the house, furniture removed to allow him to maneuver, and his bed relocated to the living room for sleeping. There were tubes and boxes everywhere, medical supplies strewn about, everything was in slings. For a woman who prided herself on cleanliness, organization, and having a tidy home, it was highly impactful on my mental health.

The daily routine for James and I changed dramatically,

becoming more complicated and increasing our stress. It took hours to get him ready for school because the simple tasks had become multifaceted. My thirty-minute routine had become ninety to one hundred minutes. I had to perform the medical procedures, bathe him, feed him, and get him to the car with his wheelchair. Then, once we arrived at school, I had to unload him and his book bag, get him into class, and try to get to work on time. I found it incredibly challenging because I was not physically able to meet the daily demands.

Suffering from insomnia, my hours of rest became even shorter as the medical procedures were conducted throughout the day and night.

Liam and William continued their routine without interruption. In fact, virtually nothing changed for them, and I doubt if they noticed the impact it was having on us.

James maintained a positive attitude, always putting on a brave face, even on the days he was frustrated with my inability to keep us on time.

There were days when I felt invisible and moments when I wanted to collapse, yet I endured. I would do anything for my children, even to my own detriment.

A visit to my doctor in October confirmed that I had diabetes and high blood pressure.

In November, my stress level grew so high that my hair and eye lashes began falling out. To add to our worries, even our dog fell ill.

By December, there was no money for Christmas gifts as James' care had devoured our pay checks.

"*Dear God, is it over yet?*"

The only way to describe that year is to say that I felt electrocuted. I was numb. I did not know how I got through it. In fact, I did not really know if it was truly over, but I know that the woman who started the year was not the same woman who finished it.

There was too much "life" in such a brief time. I began to dread getting out of bed, terrified of what the day would bring. The constant upsets and disappointments challenged my belief that life is good; my lack of rest impaired my judgement; and my ability to perform even the simplest of tasks was diminished.

How did I cope? I will never know. I put one foot in front of the other and pushed on, day in and day out. I prayed to God, cried, hoped, and kept moving.

They say you never know how strong you are until being strong is the only choice you have; how perfectly accurate.

Chapter 14

Wife and Mother – 2000s

As the months of my pregnancy flew by, Liam attended every gynecology visit, test, and examination that I had. He was excited to be a dad and I was thrilled to be a mom. He held my hand in the delivery room and never left my side.

When William was born, Liam spent every moment with him until he was out of the incubator. He loved him so much, just as he loved me. When they brought William to my room in the bassinette, I could not wait to hold him. I was so beside myself that I acted insane. I would not let anyone else touch him, including Liam. I cuddled and snuggled and breathed him in. I counted his fingers and toes. I smelled his newborn skin and kissed him. I examined every feature on his face and body. Oh, how I loved him!

Liam was equally as attentive at James' birth as he had been with William. He cradled and rocked the boys as babies, walked hours with them in the stroller, and sang to them constantly. He loved teaching them and he loved being part of a family.

The boys were our world. There are not enough words in the English dictionary to portray how much they were loved, adored, and wanted.

When William was a toddler, I would sing to him. He always loved when I sang. As he grew, I would frequently hear, "Mom, can you sing me to sleep please?" and I always did, with immense pleasure. He filled my heart with such love.

His brother, on the other hand, was a whole other story. When James was an infant, I would sing and he would howl – and I mean *howl*. He did not want any part of my singing off-key. William and I would laugh so hard. It did not matter which song I sang, James would instantly cry. Oh, I can still hear mine and William's giggles; they echo in my mind and heart.

I loved being a wife and mother; the sense of belonging to someone and being able to go home to someone. I loved sharing the abundant, deep, emotional love in my heart with my family. I loved being loved, it made me feel whole.

Adjusting to parenthood and marriage simultaneously was like driving a car and a bus at the same time, both demanded my sole attention, yet neither one received it.

Life became stressful after the babies were born, and Liam began drinking regularly as his coping mechanism.

As the bills piled high, we would borrow repeatedly, trying to stay afloat, but it became a nightmare. We owed so many people that it was embarrassing. In my world, if you owe people money, you pay them, but I simply did not have the means to do so.

I was not conditioned to being a new wife and mother. My coping strategy was prayer, and I constantly prayed for something better to come around the corner, but nothing quickly appeared.

I had no support system in my new town, unlike I did when I was home, and I was too stubborn and embarrassed to ask Mom or my family for help. It would mean acknowledging that I was a failure as a wife and mother, and I was determined to survive on my own.

Liam's family were not wealthy or as close as mine. His

father was terminally ill, the cost of his cancer medication was outrageous, and they had no insurance. They were barely able to survive themselves, they certainly could not help us.

We longed for a night out, to have a break from the stress, and went to the casino on the border of the neighboring province with a few of Liam's friends. I had never been to a casino, but his friends assured me I would enjoy it. I was grateful for the change of scenery.

Walking through the doors of the casino was overwhelming; the glitz and glamour of the room strikes you immediately as you enter. It was bright and flashy, with voices and machines ringing loudly from multiple locations.

The layout was very confusing. The carpets, with colorful red and yellow symmetrical patterns, were visually mesmerizing; there was little signage to the exits or the washrooms, making it difficult to find your way around or out of the casino. It was a tactic, I presumed, used to keep people in the casino spending their hard-earned money.

I surveyed the room slowly. There were dozens of rows of machines filled with all kinds of people, some with sad faces and some laughing, filled with excitement if they won.

Each machine had a different minimum bet, ranging from five cents to a thousand dollars. I remember thinking about how much money must be collected in a single night, and it gave me chills.

I sat down at an empty slot machine and watched the older lady next to me. I had no idea what I was supposed to do, and I eventually asked her for help. She showed me where to put my money in and how to wager a bet. I followed her instructions and the wheels on the screen started moving, sounds started beeping, and the screen started flashing. After three or four spins, everything stopped, and a light on top of the slot machine flashed red.

I calmly asked the woman what I had done to break the machine, and she laughed. "You won!" she told me.

"I won?" I responded, completely puzzled.

"Yes, you've won eight hundred dollars!" I was shocked and excited all at the same time. I rarely, if ever, won anything.

Everything I touched that night turned to gold. We won over three thousand dollars, which was astonishing considering that we arrived with ten dollars each. We headed home, thrilled with our change of luck.

As it turned out, it was the worst thing that could have ever happened. The influx of money made Liam think that this was the solution to our money problems. From that weekend on, almost every night after work, he returned to the casino; over and over, again, and again, every week going further and further into debt and never telling me. He would lie to me, saying that he had to work late, help his parents, or visit friends. I never questioned him because I trusted him.

As the bills rolled in, showing overdue payments, I would innocently ask, "Did you pay the light or gas bill?"

He would always reply, "Yes, but it was a bit late this month."

I would accept his response until the following month when I would ask again, and he would say, "Must be an error. I will call them."

Before I knew it, the bills were three months behind, and we could not pay the mortgage. We had to move out of our home and into a rented apartment. Our arguing continued, and the confrontations increased. The stress mounted as the anger and frustration grew inside me with every outright lie he told and every indiscretion he tried to cover up.

To address our constant financial shortfall, I continued to search for more suitable employment. Eventually, I found a new job in a different industry that paid more money. Shortly thereafter, I was laid off again. Liam continued gambling, and the stress increased and compounded. Panic and anxiety set in and became my normal state of being.

What was I going to do? I could not live with the stress of no money. I did not know how to handle it; I had no experience in such matters.

I recall once when I prayed feverishly, begging St. Anthony to help me find money so I could buy milk for the baby. I checked all my coat pockets and found twenty dollars. It was not much, but it was enough to get through the night.

By the end of the year, we had to look for another place to live – four moves in four years because we could not pay the rent or make ends meet. We moved to another townhouse a few blocks over; another nice, clean home. There were more deposits and fees, as we fell even further behind, and with it came more gambling, drinking, lying, frustration, requests for sex, and an increase in the chasm that grew between us.

The sex life that we'd had at the beginning of our marriage faded as the stress increased. The pressure removed all forms of intimacy, causing me to be withdrawn.

I spent many nights lying awake, wondering where the money we needed to survive was going to come from.

Finally, one night in bed, I blurted out, "I don't know what you're doing, but I'm going home."

I needed help, support, structure, and routine. I wanted my children to know the safe kind of life that I had experienced, and I surely could not provide it here. Life was a roller coaster and I just wanted off the ride.

Reluctantly, he agreed.

"I will start looking for jobs for us tomorrow."

I rolled over and faced the wall. As I lay there trying to sleep, the stress of life was getting to me. The very thing I did not want to do, I had no choice but do – I had to move in with my mother.

Defeated, I called my former boss in my hometown. We had a lengthy conversation, and she informed me that there was a job opening in management. I applied as soon as I saw it on the job board.

It did not take long for Liam to find work, and once he had secured employment, we prepared to leave. I shipped our belongings and sold many of the items that we would no longer need. We would use the furniture in Mom's house until we were able to start over. There was no money to keep our household items and put them in storage, and truthfully, the cash paid off the people we owed before we left.

By the time I moved home, I had two children, insurmountable debt, and no peace of mind. God, what a disaster! The very thing that I had been trying to avoid, I ended up doing anyway. I felt like a failure. Could matters get any worse?

As I settled into Mom's home, I realized that I was mentally ill. My dreams were shattered, and my nerves were frayed.

The stress was simply too much. I was accustomed to my family and our support network, working together as a team, truth, transparency, and honesty. I wanted a stable family life, security, beautiful things, and a beautiful home, but I did not have any of it. I had lies, deceit, debt, and uncertainty. I had gone from being meticulous about myself, my home, and my sons, to full-blown survivor mode.

The pressures of being a mother and wife were too much,

especially when coupled with the debt, Liam's drinking, and his gambling. When I came home, the focus was not on being clean and tidy. The focus was staying alive, meeting the needs of the children, and putting food on the table. I was staying with Mom because I had to, I could not survive without her.

It was a huge change for everyone. Mom had adapted to her own space and having her home meticulous. My stress level was so high that I was on edge all the time. I did not know how to deal with the financial issues that presented themselves, how to be a good mother without assistance, or how to be a loving wife.

All I knew was that I had to survive and improve life for my sweet, innocent boys. I needed the security of a home, clothes for our backs, shoes for our feet, a safe vehicle to drive in, and a job to go to. In my opinion, these were the bare necessities for any family to survive.

The stress level, as I knew it, eased with the move. I knew we would not move again unless we wanted to, and no matter what, Mom would never let us go hungry. A better job and a higher income provided a means to pay for the life that I wanted, and gradually, my stress level declined.

Mom was thrilled to have her grandbabies home and happier still to take care of them while we worked.

Now that Liam and I were bringing in a steady income, I had to remind myself that everything was going to be fine. The bills were getting paid, the debt was going down, and the children were happy. There was a light at the end of the tunnel, even if it seemed miles away.

Mom could see how stressed I was, and she never complained if I left the house in a mess – toys everywhere, dirty dishes left on the counter – she simply cleaned everything, repeatedly, with a smile. I was grateful for this gesture because I could not manage anything else.

Life was never going to let me be stress free, I should have known better.

Indebted to Mom for letting my family stay with her, I once again felt the need to find a way to repay her. She had built her own life while I was gone, and she could have told us to find an apartment.

Yes, she is my mother, but I was a grown woman with my own family, and she should not have had to take care of us. My family was my responsibility, not hers.

Gradually, I started running her errands, then cleaning her home, picking up her groceries and clothes shopping, taking her to appointments, etc. I went far beyond the role of daughter and put myself in the role of house cleaner, errand boy, butler, personal assistant – I do not know what the title would be because I filled so many roles.

Instead of healing, I was adding more responsibilities to my plate, and the fatigue grew. I had nowhere to go for a break. I did not have money to go to movies or to go out to dinner with my friends, as I had in my life prior to meeting Liam. My life consisted of home, work, and family, and the stress continued to increase without reprieve.

I was fulfilling Mom's desire to be a "princess," and this led to more challenges. She became increasingly sedentary and her ability to perform routine activities became more limited. Her health began to deteriorate, and instead of my added responsibilities being a nicety, they soon became a necessity.

What had been optional became mandatory, and as my job responsibilities increased, what I could not do fell to Liam. He had to mow the lawns, paint the house, run the errands, and be available for her every whim. I do not mean to sound ungrateful, because she was an older woman with health issues, but by catering to her needs, she became spoiled and often unreasonably demanding.

It was by far one of the most painstaking, and necessary, actions that I had to take, but it destroyed Liam. He had been on his own since he was eighteen years old, and he enjoyed the life that he had built, making solo decisions, and living on his own salary. He was not prepared for the expectations that came with being a husband and a father, the demands that I made on his time, or the responsibilities that came with having a family. He did not understand me, or my needs, wants, and desires. He only knew the single mindset, which is how he was raised.

Frankly, I did not see what was happening to him. We did not talk about the move and how it impacted him. I just assumed he would be as relieved and as happy as I was to have some sense of security, but he was not. It made him resentful; he did not feel like a man. I had inadvertently emasculated him.

He wanted to provide for us but was unable. He had dug himself a hole so big that he could not see a way out, and his anger and disappointment in himself grew. He compared himself to my family members, who were educated and successful, and, I believe, he felt he did not measure up.

Living with Mom and the added responsibilities was too much pressure for him to bear. We could be in the middle of having sex when Mom would call up and ask for something, and if we did not answer, she would start banging on the walls to get our attention. Or in the middle of a discussion about the kids, and she would call out for assistance. It became insufferable.

It was never my intention to stay with Mom for any length of time. I wanted to save money and get our own home in the province that I knew and loved but life was not going to let me have it.

As the stress peaked from the poor decisions that we'd made, the abuse started. Name calling, digs about the past, small insignificant things at first, then progressing to confusing emotional mind games.

Liam began making snide comments when I would wear new clothes to work. *"Who are you dressing up for today?"*

Initially, I would laugh, thinking he was teasing and meant it as a complement.

You see, I only had eyes for him and everything in my purview was framed in that perspective. I wanted my family to work, and I would not jeopardize it in any way. I would kiss and hug him frequently, reassuring him that I loved him, but the derogatory comments continued.

When I could afford it, I bought fashionable and sexy clothing, like tight fitting leggings or pretty tops with V-necks. Yes, you could see some cleavage, but I did not have my breasts boldly on display.

"Isn't that a little much to be wearing for work?" he would sneer.

"It's in style," I would reply. Then he would pour himself a coffee and sulk as I went out the door.

He had become so accustomed to seeing me haggard, in old clothes and without makeup, that when I started to care for myself again, he assumed it was because I was looking for, or interested in, someone else, which was not the case. I wanted to regain my self-esteem. I thought it would make him proud to have his wife look as good as when he met her, but the opposite was true. In his mind, caring for myself was the equivalent of saying I am looking for someone to replace you.

I thought it was a passing phase, but the behavior continued far longer than I thought it would. I was in shock, *who was this man?* I did not know him. Where was the man that I had married – the kind, loving, thoughtful, and considerate man?

I would learn, over the course of our marriage, that Liam was a Dr. Jekyll and Mr. Hyde. Some days, he was the most kind, loving man on the planet, but the days when his insecurities became too much to deal with, I would find myself face to face with the dark Mr. Hyde.

He continued dredging up the past, asking about old boyfriends. Who was here in my hometown that I had dated or been with? Who was coming to steal me away? It became monotonous, and honestly, I thought he was losing his mind. Anyone in my past had no place in my present or future.

Being truthful and transparent, I shared my history with him, assuming it would calm him, but it was a huge mistake. He only wanted to use it as ammunition against me, to make me feel bad, unwanted, and unworthy. And it was highly effective, because I was losing who I was; I was losing faith in me.

He isolated me from my friends and made me rethink every relationship. I did not go anywhere with anyone. I would not dare look at or speak to men, always walking with my head down. I was only "allowed" around women. Male friends would say "hi," and I would smile weakly, fearful of his reaction. I simplified my life by going to work and coming immediately home at the end of the day. My time was solely spent with him and the boys.

In retrospect, I realize that he was simply deflecting his issues onto me; anything to take the blame off himself and his feelings. He had not learned appropriate coping mechanisms to deal with his frustrations and internal emotional turmoil. He knew what he was doing was wrong, emotionally lashing out and hurting me, but he continued the behavior because it was the only method he knew to relieve his pain and anger. Making me feel bad made him feel better because then we were both miserable.

He wanted to control and manipulate me, and he did, but I did not see it – for years. I was too busy trying to please and pacify him, provide for the kids and be happy. I was too busy trying to live. I had no idea what he was doing was coercive control, and no inkling that it was a form of abuse. I simply thought it was life.

Friday night was grocery night. He loved to find a good bargain and he enjoyed shopping, so I would stay home and entertain the kids, my favorite pastime.

He would be gone for hours, but I never questioned his absence because he would arrive home with plenty of food and supplies. Over time, the quantity of groceries dwindled, due in part to the cost of living and because he found other ways to spend his money. He would unpack his purchases and then say he forgot something and leave again. I did not think too much of it. Anyone can forget items, can't they?

The first night that he did not come home until three a.m. I was frantic. I was calling him repeatedly on his phone without a response. A million thoughts went through my mind. Had he been in a car accident? Was he out with someone else? I lay in bed thinking of every God-awful thing that could have happened to him and tortured myself until I heard the loud creak of the door. I jumped out of bed and went running to him, inquiring if everything was okay, relieved that he was safe.

He was fully inebriated, barely able to stand, staggering as he walked. His eyes were blood red and the smell of alcohol on his breath was overpowering; his clothes wreaked of cigarette smoke. I stared at him in disbelief and then stormed angrily back to bed, fuming. *How could he do this to me? Didn't he think I would worry*? It was very inconsiderate.

When he woke, he made up a story about how he bumped into a friend from work, had a few drinks, and lost track of time.

In the moment, I believed him and excused the behavior because I wanted to trust him. I would not accept that I had married a man who would intentionally deceive me, and I certainly did not expect it to happen again.

Within two weeks, the same set of events occurred. There was no phone call to say where he was or what he was doing to alleviate my fears. There was more worrying and wondering, and then the behavior began repeating; first Fridays, then Saturdays too.

Every time I would confront him, he would that say he needed to relieve his stress, and I would lie to protect the children. Family time and being together after all week was not cutting it for him, and the illusion I had built around him and my perfect life continued to crumble.

Mom's demands increased. She never respected our decisions, our relationship, or the fact that I was a married woman. In her eyes, I was still her baby girl. It was about what she needed, and she always needed something. My sense of obligation to her for her constant selflessness made it impossible for me to refuse.

Liam was frequently yelling about money, the kids, work, living with Mom, the weather, my clothes, family, neighbors – the subject did not matter. He found fault with everything and everyone because he was so unhappy. He could not see the forest for the trees, wanting out of the mess but unsure how to get there.

Our arguments escalated; we argued about his behavior and the dirty habits that I had hoped we'd left in the past. The drinking that had temporarily subsided when we first had the children now became more frequent. He found a few local bars, which had lottery gambling machines, and began patronizing them on a regular basis to get away from the constant demands on his time. I watched the money quickly drain from our bank account and wondered where it was going.

The money allocated to pay down debt was suddenly disappearing. When I confronted him, he admitted that he was gambling again, and I was shattered. I begged him to let me take over the management of our finances, but he refused, saying that I could do no better than he could.

Dismayed by his behavior, I began thinking to myself, *I am never going to get my own space or have a secure future*. Although he stated that he wanted out of mom's house, his actions very clearly indicated otherwise.

This was *my* husband, the man I *chose* to marry. I prayed, hoping the worst was surely over.

I was focused on raising my sons, having them educated, giving them a home, introducing them to good friends and neighbors, and keeping them out of trouble; I did not have time to raise a man too. I needed a partner, not another child; someone to lean on and lean with.

The behavior continued, even if I did not recognize it as abuse at the time. It was mental abuse and emotional mind games, not physical abuse, so I did not see it for what it was.

I honestly believe that Liam did not mean to be this way. Burned by his first girlfriend who cheated on him, he had huge trust issues. He did not know how to soothe and comfort me, or how to manage his many insecurities. Raised in a difficult environment, I attributed his behavior to his family life.

Optimistic that he could heal, and we could grow together, I continued to drown him in love, never believing that circumstances would get worse.

One night, he had been drinking hard alcohol – dark rum – and he was sarcastic and cold. His behavior was unpredictable, and it made me nervous.

Wanting to avoid an argument, I went to bed early. I had been asleep for a couple of hours when I felt him climb into bed, his cold hands touching my body. I pushed his hands away, telling him that I wanted to sleep, but he was insistent. I refused.

Upset with my response, he took the drink he had brought to bed and threw it at the wall, shattering the crystal glass. The liquid splattered and ran down the wall in slow motion, like rain on a windowpane.

I jumped from the bed, my heart pounding, my body shaking. Wanting protection, I went running to the boys' room to get away from him. Though there was nothing they could do to help me, I knew he would never hurt them, and I felt safe there. I shut the bedroom door and sat quietly on the floor, watching them sleep, while I waited for the pacing to stop and the silence to arrive.

After hours of listening for noise and footsteps, I eventually fell asleep.

The next day, he was extremely remorseful, but I could not and did not want to look at him. He attempted to wrap his arms around me while I was cooking in the kitchen, but I shook him off as he kept repeating, "I am sorry. Deeply sorry. It will never happen again. Please forgive me."

Words failed me.

I could have regurgitated. I simply could not reconcile how the man that I loved could do this to me. He was my *husband*; he is supposed to *protect* me not *endanger* me. I was so angry with him, and in that moment, for the first time in our marriage, I hated him for what he was doing to me, to us, and to our future.

Anger, for me, is a pointless waste of energy, and I have never harbored it for long. Instead, I offered forgiveness, ignored my boundaries, and let him cross into unchartered territory. And with every subsequent act of betrayal and degradation, I lost more of myself as I constantly reset my boundaries, unknowingly inching closer to my breaking point.

Of course, it did not help that the bad times were always intermingled with the good. His unpredictable behavior could go on for weeks and then, suddenly cease when his tension was released. It reminded me of a boiling kettle, screaming until you turn it off.

Then the man that I had married would reappear, filled with remorse and love. He would take me to dinner, shopping, buy me roses and treat me like a queen. He allowed me to see my husband as I envisioned him, giving me hope for the future.

He came to church with me, dressed fashionably, and enrolled in courses to further his education.

He was a great cook and a diligent worker, never shying away from overtime or part-time jobs to provide for his family, despite the funds that he allocated to his unhealthy habits.

He loves his children without exception; there is nothing that he would not do for them. He would sacrifice repeatedly if it meant that it would help the kids or provide for their needs.

He provided them direction and guidance based on the lessons that he had learned in his life.

He has been helpful to my family and friends, assisting them with their needs whenever asked, and without being asked. He is intelligent and frequently took the children to events and museums to educate them.

"Good Liam" would stay for weeks, sometimes months, and

every time he did appear, I would fall in love with him all over again. We would attend family gatherings, go on picnics together, have date nights, and private intimate time together to rebuild and repair our relationship.

On the days that "good Liam" arrived home first, housework was non-existent. The cooking, cleaning, and laundry would be completed by the time I arrived, and together time would become a priority.

Kind words flowed from his lips and gentleness from his hands.

Liam would ensure that we had family time with the boys – game nights, video games, playing hide and seek, or just chasing each other around the house. On those days, I loved him more than I could express.

Such is the roller coaster of abuse. The same "calm-tension building-incident-reconciliation" cycle that Amanda had experienced was also prevalent in my own home, though I was oblivious to it.

It was those "good days" that offered hope and created a false belief that my love could change him. I could clearly see that he was not all bad, and that he made an effort to change. That pattern of behavior and thinking kept me holding on, preventing me from realizing that I was a victim of abuse.

I cannot count the number of times that he has said "it will never happen again," and each time, I would fill with hope and pray that he was telling the truth. I wanted desperately to believe him. When you love someone, and they promise to change, it's normal to believe them, even if experience has taught you otherwise. Hope is truly omnipotent.

The roller coaster of ups and downs, faith and despair, tether you to the relationship. Keeping the peace, ultimately, becomes a method for psychological survival.

Upon reflection, I should have walked out the door that day and never looked back. Perhaps I should have gone long before, but I did not want my kids to come from a broken home. I wanted, what I had never had growing up, a family that was whole, so I stayed.

I did not realize at the time that I was choosing an abusive home over a broken one. I did not have the presence of mind to see the abuse, or how it was affecting my thoughts and rationale. I never considered the long-term impact that this decision would have on myself or my children. Though there were times that I considered leaving, I did not think that I could survive on my own. And if I left, how he would survive?

I had been primed, to put his needs and the needs of my children ahead of my own. I could not bear the thought of causing my sons pain. I completely ignored the turmoil that he was putting me through, rationalizing that my presence, even if I was falling apart, was better than my absence.

My mind continuously offered a million excuses to stay. The justifying and reasoning were a defense mechanism to keep sane and help me cope with daily life. It is amazing how the human mind can fabricate a mountain of excuses explaining away bad behavior to make everything "normal" and acceptable.

To make the relationship work, you strategize every word spoken, and every action taken, attempting to prevent the abuse from ever occurring, believing that you can control another person's behavior and emotions.

You convince yourself that you will never discuss the past or say things that will trigger his feelings of inferiority again; you will never give him a reason to say those hostile words or demean you ever again; but it is a delusion.

You cannot walk on eggshells and live in such an anxious, unforgiving state for the rest of your life. The only thing you control is *your* words, thoughts, and actions.

His phases of gambling, drinking, questioning, subtle intimidation, and fear went on for more than twenty years. They would repeat every six months or so – sometimes every six weeks.

His insecurities devoured him, and his demeaning ways ate away at my soul. It destroyed me, piece by piece, obliterating the line between acceptable and unacceptable behavior, until I no longer recognized myself.

I never understood it. I wanted to live in the moment and focus on the present, but his roots were solidly anchored in the past.

I grew to hate it, and eventually, being alone with him – something I had loved – became something that I dreaded.

It made me fearful, overwhelmed, and weary. It was mentally draining, and it served no purpose other than to tear me down.

There were many warning signs that I ignored because I did not *want* to see them. I wanted a perfect life and happy family. I believed that my love would be strong enough to change him, to teach him, and to turn him into the diamond I desired, but I could not have been more wrong.

He often asked me why I dated Mr. X or Mr. Y. How could I do that to him? I was confused by his questions. "Do what to you? I never knew you existed then. I did not do anything to you. I was looking for a husband," I would say.

It seemed that he was trying to erase my life before him, to make me his, and his alone. He never seemed to understand that those failed relationships, and the lessons they had taught me, had shaped me into the woman that he loved.

I sometimes think that he is more to be pitied than blamed. Since birth, life has been a struggle for him. When he was a child, his father would drink, and his mother would take them to the barn to sleep and protect them. She wrapped them in tarps to keep them warm, telling them that they were playing a game because they could not get in the house. It must have affected him, though he rarely discusses his childhood and the events that transpired. He only hints that it was not filled with many good memories.

I genuinely believed that I had enough love in me to fix him and make him shine. I tried to piece him back together and make him whole, but I did not realize I was emptying myself and ignoring my own needs to do it. I didn't notice how much I was giving and how much he was taking. There was no balance; it was completely one-sided.

I never realized the impact that it could have. I had never encountered a person who took so much before, or a person who needed so much. When I was home with Mom, we all gave and received, which is why we all grew, even if it was in different directions.

All I wanted was a normal, loving, marital relationship, but normal was never going to happen.

Part 2

Chapter 15

Home – 2010s

I started tracking the amount of money he was squandering, and the next time he complained about not having our own space, I presented my findings. "If you stop spending money and start saving it, we can buy our own house," I told him.

The shock of seeing the amount of money he had wasted must have reached some part of him, because he finally started working with me. It was the first time in our then ten-year marriage that we were on the same page.

Eighteen months later, we moved into our beautiful new home in one of the hottest real estate markets located in the west end of the city. A three-story home with a level backyard and a two-car driveway.

Although we were both listed as owners, I took great comfort in knowing that I was making the payments without him. My children and I needed security; I would not and could not lose it.

To me, it represented winning, surviving, and getting back on my feet. It is why the house meant so much to me; it was like a prize at the end of an exhausting marathon.

On the day we moved in, friends and family were surprised, as no one expected it or even knew about it. I had not told a soul that I was trying for it, in the event that it did not work out or life took it away.

I managed to cross the finish line, though, and provided my

children with their own home.

Time in this house was more positive and far less nerve-racking, as we made attempts to restore our marriage and rebuild our relationship. The kids met new friends and participated in extracurricular activities, such as hockey, karate, baseball, swimming, music lessons, and soccer. Liam puttered away in his garage and his pride slowly began to return.

Over time, things improved financially. We travelled to Florida, New York, California, and across Canada and to visit our respective families. Liam and I took the kids to Disney World, and we thrived on our time spent with the boys. They developed their mother's passion for travel and seeing new things, and their father's adventurous spirit for trying new things.

Family vacations were sheer bliss. Time away from our routine life, provided a needed change of scenery. We went sightseeing and to the water parks, rode the waterslides, roller coaster rides, and go carts. William, James, and I played in the wave pool. I threw them up in the air and let them fall into the water, screaming and giggling with excitement.

They were shocked. I had always been sad and grumpy mommy, they had rarely seen happy and fun mommy, and they loved this side of me. We giggled and laughed, and I was thrilled to make such happy memories. We ate ice cream, hamburgers, and French fries. We were a family who went everywhere and did everything together.

Our trip to Disney World was filled with love and laughter. We spent days by the pool, where the children would jump and swim until nightfall. They were engrossed in wrestling at the time, and would frequently pose, trying to imitate John Cena, Rey Mysterio, and the Undertaker.

They would suck in their tummies and raise their arms,

trying to flex their biceps, attempting to mimic the famous poses. Of course, at their youthful age, they didn't have much in the way of muscle mass. They created their own fan club of tourists around the pool who giggled and applauded after each of their performances.

We visited Cinderella's castle where they met Mickey Mouse, the Chipmunks, Goofy, Minnie Mouse, and Buzz Lightyear. We collected badges and pins to wear in memory of our time at the park. They oohed and aahed at the dramatic fireworks display and watched earnestly as Tinkerbell flew through the night air, awed by the magic of flight. They went on a safari in Animal Kingdom, and cluttered their cameras with pictures of lions, tigers, hippos, and giraffes.

Every morning, they would run to the restaurant and gobble down chocolate chip pancakes, bacon, and juice; then, they would run back to the pool to deliver another performance. They thought they were in paradise, and they never wanted to leave. Life was good, time was kind, and love was plentiful.

Life stabilized for four years. The abuse continued, but much less frequently, and finally, my mental health began to improve. At last, I could relax and breathe, the ride had paused. The kids grew and changed schools; James went to high school, and William prepared for university. For a brief time, life resembled normal.

Little did I know that the years of struggle I had endured were in preparation for 2016, the summit of the worst year of my life.

Chapter 16

Healing James – 2017

The focus, in 2017, was solely on making James better. We wanted to get him walking, and moving and to try to return to normal. Time flew so fast, that year went by in a blur.

My job was very demanding, and the downtime made for even longer hours, though I was grateful for the flexibility and the time to address James' care. We played video and board games, went for walks, and tried to stay active. We did everything we could to keep his mood upbeat.

Nominated as the Children's Hospital Miracle Child in 2017, James is a remarkable child and an inspiration to others. He does not let his condition affect him psychologically or hinder him from leading a positive social and physical life. At the end of the school year, he was honored by his junior high school with a perseverance award to recognize his grit, determination, and dedication despite the obstacles he faced.

In September 2017, James started high school. I knew he was feeling pressure when, on the first day of school, he vomited before we even stepped outside the door.

High school is difficult enough when you are normal, let alone when you have a disability. James was worried about how his friends would treat him, and about how he would survive in a bigger school with triple the student population.

The teachers were kind and reached out prior to start of the school year to arrange a tour for James. They also ensured that James' classrooms were in close proximity to each other. The school was large, with four floors, a lot of stairs, and only one elevator.

James, much like me, has a stubborn streak, and his pride prevented him from taking the elevator. Wanting to be like everyone else, he chose the stairs frequently.

By the end of the day, his energy was depleted. I would frequently explain that he needed to use the elevator, not because of weakness, but to alleviate the stress that the significant amount of walking was putting on his body. Being a teenager, he ignored me, which frustrated me.

Fortunately, schoolwork kept his mind occupied. It was exactly the kind of reprieve he needed from the poking and investigating that was taking place in the hospital. He wanted desperately to be normal; I would have done anything to grant his wish.

By the end of the year, he had accepted his new circumstances and, thankfully, his childhood friends remained his long-term friends through high school. They helped and encouraged him. With their support, he gradually relaxed and adjusted to his new surroundings.

As our new normal began to take hold, I paused to collect myself and regain my bearings. I had been pummeled by life and was struggling to adjust. My age did not help, as menopause decided to arrive at the same time.

Truthfully, it was utter madness. Between the mood changes, hot flashes, night sweats, and sleeping problems, I was a wreck. My mind was muddy, and my thoughts were scattered like leaves on a windy day. There were times when I did not know if I was coming or going; I was simply trying to survive.

I could not process the overwhelming amount of information flowing through my brain. I often found myself mindlessly scrolling through social media, looking at the faces of people I did not know, wondering if any of them had experienced this kind of strife and emotional upheaval in their lives.

I began questioning my life, marriage, and state of happiness. I slowly realized that I had grown apart from my husband.

Despite the support offered by my friends throughout this ordeal, I needed my husband, but his support seemed non-existent. It certainly did not meet my expectations of it. In my mind, he was oblivious to the toll that these events were having on James and me. He seemed lost in his own thoughts, trying to find his own coping strategies.

I felt alone in my devastation and, when I needed to lean, there was no one to lean on. My views of life, people and myself changed; I was not the same person as before. I felt weary and drained. All. The. Time.

There seemed to be no reprieve from life. *It is not meant to be this convoluted and problematic, is it?*

Liam offered me no time for comfort, empathy, or connection. While I recognize that everyone deals with tragedy and grief in their own way, I always thought that it would bring us closer together, but these events did not seem to impact his routine or change anything in his world.

To this day, I do not know if he is aware of how significantly they impacted me.

I just existed. I breathed in and out, and my heart beat, but for all intents and purposes, that was it. I was not present, I was not aware; I was robotic. I was drowning in despair and gasping for air.

I had no idea how much was missing in my marriage until the craters in my soul were filled by the most unlikely people, and in the most unusual way.

As the fog in my mind began to clear, a light shone on the reality that Liam was not who I had made him out to be. I uncovered a darkness in our marriage that I had been unaware of before. The dream life that I was pretending to have did not exist, and with every passing day, this reality became more transparent.

In late 2017, a friend introduced to me to Instagram. Unfamiliar with the software, I experimented with it and began receiving messages from strangers in this new, online world. Me being me, I was friendly and sweet to everyone I met. If someone was nice to me, I reciprocated.

Life is so unpredictable. You never know when you are going to meet someone who can change your life. I could not have imagined how one innocent conversation with a stranger would lead to the complete annihilation of every ounce of peace I knew.

Chapter 17

Easter – 2018

I managed to keep my tattered and torn life together for another year and kept moving forward. James attended classes and worked toward his high school diploma, and though he rarely went outside the house after the paralysis, his friends never left his side.

Our dog, Storm, provided comfort and became his best friend. She entertained him with tricks and her crazy behavior, chasing light beams and tossing her toys in the air. She brought him laughter and a source of exercise as he chased her around the house.

William continued to date Sarah, though he now spent less time at home. He preferred to be socializing with her and their friends, as any teenager would. They were both accepted into the Engineering Faculty and, together, worked toward graduating and building a future for themselves.

Despite the attempts to reconcile and repair our relationship, Liam and I continued to drift apart because I had not been honest with him or myself. I had been pretending that life was fine when it was not. I did not have the courage to communicate the damage he had done, or the pain I was feeling, fearing backlash. Instead of understanding that I was not solely responsible, I carried the weight of the relationship on my shoulders, and I began to cave under its massive weight.

On Easter Sunday, in a rare moment of silence when the drama slowed, I took time to reflect upon the years of my marriage, my previous relationships, and love.

It was an awakening. I realized that every experience I had had with love starkly contrasted with its meaning. I had tried to be a living example of the empathy and vulnerability which define it, but, as I stared into the wood-trimmed mirror that hung on the bathroom wall, I realized that the woman who had been the epitome of love was now emaciated from the lack of it.

I examined my reflection. Time had been kind to me, even if life had not. I looked like I was in my forties, ten years younger than my actual age. I had a few wrinkles on my face, but nothing which expressed the hardship that I had endured. At five foot seven, my curvy figure outlined the fact that I was a mother.

As my dyed-blonde hair glistened under the vanity light, tears began streaming from my eyes, black mascara tracing a path down my face.

How did I end up here? I wondered.

There was no resemblance to the woman I had been in my twenties. That young woman, accustomed to middle class luxury, was now full of scars and stretch marks – inside and out. The sense of self-esteem and pride I had known was non-existent.

I glanced out the window, my mind riddled with confusion, flooded with thoughts and memories from the past, my current grief-stricken state overwhelming me. It was a beautiful spring day, but like I had many times in the past few years, I wanted to crawl back into bed. I had given up and wanted to die. I was tired of contemplating ways to address the nightmare that my life had become. I was filled with regret for the decisions I had made, and for not living the life I wanted.

In living life to please others, I had lost myself and my

bearings. I did not know who I was, what I wanted, or how to proceed. Uncertain of my path, I considered letting my life fall apart. Trying to hold it all together had become an impossible task. *How much worse could it get?*

Unable to think clearly, I felt paralyzed, as if walking through a field of land mines. I feared that my future decisions would be worse than those in the past, and I was terrified the next step would be my last. At fifty-three, I could not afford any further missteps.

As I dressed for the day, Liam entered, spouting his sarcastic comments and demeaning me. Never directly, always taunting in a way that I knew what he meant even though the children did not. I was tired of listening to his derogatory comments when they were untrue, but he was relentless.

As he left the room for a moment, the pain, which had lain dormant for years, erupted like a volcano.

I stared at my reflection, repeating quietly to myself, "Hold on, just hold on. You will get through this. You're strong, you can get through anything. You've made it this far."

But the words seemed hollow, and the image of the woman staring back at me from the mirror was unrecognizable. She was nothing but a shell, lost and defeated. Unable to look at myself any longer, I retreated to the bedroom.

Powerless to stop the release of pent-up angst and years of heartache, my shoulders shook as my head fell into my hands. My body collapsed into the air-filled duvet on the bed, and the tears flowed like a broken dam.

Liam returned and stared at me blankly. "I did not mean anything by it. I am not trying to start something," he said, but I knew it wasn't true. This was our normal.

In that moment, I ceased believing in love or hoping for

happiness, and any remnants of hope that I had, any belief of happiness for the future, left and never returned.

I pulled myself together, dried my tears, and went for a drive – my energy drained, my thoughts empty, my heart empty, my expression devoid of emotion.

On that day, I knew, our marriage was over.

I snapped like a rubber band pushed beyond its limits, fracturing, unable to return to its previous state. I realized nothing was going to change. The pain that had existed since the early days of our marriage was always going to be there.

He finally broke me, my spirit, my belief in humanity and love. I would never be the same.

Weeks later, while driving home after a particularly rough day at work, I started to cry. "Lord, I can't do this anymore," I said aloud. When I had married, I believed it would be for life, but surely this is not what would be in store for me? Abuse and mental torture?

"I love you, Lord, but I can't do this anymore. I'm so sorry if I let you down, but I just can't. Please, Lord, help me find a man who will love me and genuinely appreciate me for me. I'm begging you, Lord!" I screamed out in the empty car. "Please, Lord, please!" Tears poured out of my eyes and down my face as I aimlessly drove home, my heart in pieces.

A week or so later, the same thing happened, and I repeated the same prayer. This time I added, "I need him now, Lord, or I'm not going to survive."

I decided that I had to unburden myself. I sat down with Liam and mumbled, "We have to talk." I sat on the couch, he in his leather chair. I began sobbing uncontrollably, "I'm unhappy. There is something missing in my life and in our marriage. I feel incredibly sad and alone."

I expected him to come to me, wrap his arms around me, and offer words of reassurance. It would be the decent thing to do, wouldn't it?

"Well then, go have an affair, and get it out of your system," he muttered. I gasped in disbelief. *Get what out of my system? My need for love, affection, and attention?* I thought.

How do you reply to something like that? This was the man I loved, the one person in the world who was supposed to love and care for me until death. In that moment, I felt like I meant nothing to him; I was merely an inconvenience.

It was just more of the same, it is all he has ever thought of me. I should never have expected anything different; he never listened to me or understood what I meant. It was his insecurities responding again.

Unaware of my movements, I walked away, eyes wide open, my mind processing a million thoughts at once, yet not fully comprehending what was happening around me.

Chapter 18

Surviving

From then on, I filled my spare time with my phone in my hand, surfing the web, and scrolling through social media. I could not handle anything else; I was broken and couldn't think straight. I felt… nothing.

Then, one day, while online, I met Daniel Ian Wilkinson. An engineer working in the United Kingdom and living in the United States; he was handsome, had a great smile, white teeth, graying hair, and deep brown eyes. He was well groomed, intelligent, and successful.

Our conversations were casual; we discussed family, work, and our extracurricular activities. I was not looking for love, I could not handle love. I was not looking for sex. I was looking to fill the emotional crater that existed within me. I was looking for a friend, someone who would listen, be sympathetic and supportive, and someone I could lean on for a pause, a break, from life. I needed someone with whom I could share my grief, someone who would provide solace.

He offered all of that and more. He was sweet, kind, tender, thoughtful, romantic, and loving. He called and texted multiple times a day, every day. He lavished me with attention, and he won me – hook, line, and sinker. I was falling in love, and he was falling in love with me.

It is difficult to explain what he did and how he did it, but somehow, he filled every emotional crack and crevice within me. My sadness and loneliness disappeared. He made me feel beautiful, loved, wanted, cared for, and appreciated. He valued my thoughts and opinions, and he consulted with me about his work and daily struggles.

He sent romantic messages and emotional voicemails, and even sent flowers to my work. The time I spent with him made me the happiest woman on the planet. I fell deeply and madly in love with him and the beautiful façade he had created. For a woman who lacked love, support, and connection, it was as if I had won the lottery.

The infatuation and illusion of a relationship went on for months. Hearing his voice sent me soaring into the clouds, and seeing the pictures from his daily life made me feel a part of it. I made time in my day, every day, to speak with him and text him, no matter how demanding my schedule.

Little did I know how blatantly obvious my change in behavior had become. The days we spoke, I was joyful; the days we did not, I was almost intolerable. Nothing in my world seemed to be right without him. It was as if my soul had been starving and he was nourishing it back to life.

I am not certain if it was because I was vulnerable or because I had been so unhappy, but whatever the reason, Daniel made me realize that there was more out there for me. There was more than I had, and more that I wanted; more respect, more love, and better emotional connections. I wanted it all.

I contemplated leaving my husband, my home, and my life in the hope of receiving the love I desperately sought.

I shared our online relationship with my closest friends, who were reluctant and hesitant to believe me. They were concerned with my abrupt change in behavior, and the speed at which I was falling in love, saying, "Kate, please be careful."

Months later, they asked if I had spoken to him on FaceTime. "No, we still have not done a video. His camera is broken," I told them nonchalantly.

My friends restated, "He is not real. No one's camera is broken for months, Kate. Think about it."

They warned me, repeatedly, citing numerous cases of women all over the world being conned by men and being scammed out of thousands of dollars, but I was so in love, so infatuated, that I did not want to believe them. I chose to believe that this was the man God had sent to answer my prayers for help, and therefore, they had to be wrong.

Having filled my mind with doubt, I googled and googled, searched and searched. Nothing abnormal. He had to be real; I could not find anything out of the ordinary.

I argued with them, telling them that they were wrong about him, explaining there was no indication that there was anything suspicious. A few more months passed.

"No, he's not asking for money. Yes, we are still talking."

"He's trying to con you," they replied.

"You're being ridiculous," I told them. *He has to be real,* I thought to myself.

I continued googling and searching, until the day I found it. It was his picture with a different name. I froze. My heart stopped beating and I ceased breathing, as if time stood still.

I shook my head. *It can't be!* I thought. It was.

My body shivered in shock as I stared at the face of the man I loved, who was now a total, complete stranger. My eyes shifted in slow motion, from the screen to the cold gray walls, in sheer disbelief as my heart turned to stone.

I felt like such a fool, as another hole was bored into and

removed from my soul, another piece of me given away to a man who did not deserve it.

The sense of emptiness and despair I had known all too well bubbled to the surface as tears rolled down my cheeks, the taste of salt lingering on my lips. *Oh God, please, no, don't do this to me. Please, I cannot take any more pain. Haven't I been through enough?*

Having been at the office when I discovered this, I put away what I was working on, collected my belongings, and crept out the rear door of the department, my head down. I was unable to speak, my mind unable to form sentences, my mouth unable to find words. I was devastated.

The picture was of an architect from Montreal. Daniel was a con artist, a fake, a liar. Like so many women before me, I had fallen in love with a con. There have been hundreds, if not thousands, of us who have fallen for their antics.

Oh. My. God.

I was ready to give up my family, my life, to go to a man who did not exist. After everything I had been through, everything I had endured, fate played yet another cruel trick on me. I was not going anywhere. He did not love me. He did not want me. It was all lies.

It ripped me apart.

I had nothing left in me; the well was bone dry.

Nothing. No one.

Rock bottom.

I confronted him, and he questioned where I found the picture. "On the Internet," I hissed. I cussed, swore, and spewed every nasty word and phrase I could think of at him. He asked me to calm down so that he could explain.

"Daniel, there is nothing to explain. You are a liar and a con artist."

"Kate, I am still the same man; the man you fell in love with. What difference does it make if I do not look like that? I love you, Kate. I know you love me."

I slammed the phone down on the counter, enraged. He was right, I did love him. It did not matter what he looked like, but it mattered that he lied to me. If I were going to start over, I could not live with, or survive, another life filled with deceit.

My phone vibrated with an incoming text message.

"I'll miss you, Kate. I love you," he texted.

"No, you don't, Daniel! You never loved me," I replied.

Then, in an instant, he was gone. The account deleted, contact information and conversation erased, no numbers, no way to locate or connect.

Just, gone.

The woman who always had faith and believed in people, she died that day. The woman who wanted and needed love no longer existed. The culmination of years of abuse, lack of love, and ultimate betrayal resulted in the first time in my life that I contemplated suicide. My heart could not take any more pain.

I could not take another step. I just couldn't.

Chapter 19

Dust Yourself Off

Hurting someone you do not know is as easy as sitting on the bank of a river, skimming a rock across the surface of the water. However, you never know how far the rock will go, the ripple effect it will have, or how much pain your actions may cause the other person.

How could I get back up? Where could I find the energy to dust myself off and try again? I did not know what to do or where to turn, because the darkness had swallowed me whole.

I messaged the man he was pretending to be to advise that his picture was in circulation and being used to defraud women. He was truly kind and responded with an apology, feeling terrible for the pain I had endured, and acknowledging it was out of his control.

It was not his responsibility to apologize; he was just being compassionate. Sadly, he was all too familiar with these circumstances as his picture had been used countless times in multiple fraud attempts.

I went to Instagram and the FBI and reported him. It did not matter what I did or who I turned to, no one could soothe the pain of my raw, open wound. I sought comfort and reassurance, but there was nothing but more pain. My soul was hemorrhaging from the daggers thrust into it, with no way to stop the bleeding.

With nowhere to turn, out of habit, I went to my husband seeking comfort, but he was cold and detached.

I decided to go to my mother and sister, surely, they would understand. I explained my behavior, and expressed my dismay about Liam and the abuse, about Daniel, and my unhappiness. The response? Mom told me to go home to my husband; I was a married woman. My sister agreed.

My jaw dropped; I was speechless. How could they not understand or even care about what I was going through? I felt unloved, unwanted, alone, insignificant, and invisible. The pain grew in intensity the waves of grief and desperation pounded the shores of my heart.

This was my family, the people I turned to in times of trouble, the people I had emotionally supported throughout my entire life. The mother whose wounds I had bandaged daily for months when she was unable to care for herself, while at the same time caring for my son and physically exhausted myself. The woman whose house I had cleaned and whose errands I had run daily. The sister I had confided in since I was a child.

I ached in places I did not know existed inside me. I staggered to the door and did not return for months. I had mustered all my energy to get the courage to tell them, because I had hidden it for so long, but there was no support for me, no sense of understanding or compassion, just more expectations.

In my opinion, their focus was on the potential loss of Liam and how it would impact them, as opposed to supporting me, my well-being, and my mental health.

Being in love with your dream man, assuming he loves and feels the same way about you, then discovering it is all a lie, makes you question *everything*. Trust in yourself and others is eradicated. You no longer trust your thought process, decision making, or your ability to cope. The perception of life, that was once dependable, becomes uncertain because you cannot reconcile how this could happen to you.

Sleep became non-existent as I went to bed every night examining every detail of every failed relationship. I wondered what I did wrong and what I could have changed to make it better. Why did I ignore the red flags? How did I allow myself to be so trusting?

Every night, you beat yourself up and wonder what you could have done differently, holding yourself responsible for your actions, as well as those outside of your control, knowing full well there is no changing it.

You try to convince yourself that life will get better and hope that, somehow, the years of your life spent with the wrong person will miraculously be restored. You pray to be given a chance to relive and correct it. You hope that the pieces of your soul that you lost and gave away will return, and miraculously make you whole again.

As the weeks passed, the pain became intolerable, and I did not want to live another day because I could not see an end in sight. Everything in and around me felt dark and hopeless. I believed that I was nothing more than an annoyance, a person who should not exist.

The rain poured from the heavens as the tears streamed from my eyes, making it difficult to see. Driving home from work had become something I dreaded because I did not know what or who I would be facing when I arrived. Work was my sanity, my place of safety.

I was almost home when I pulled over to compose myself, unable to stop my body from trembling in despair.

It was dusk, and I felt very alone. I prayed to God, but the only audible sound was the rain on the car roof, as if heaven was crying for my thoughts and the deeds in my mind.

I thought about the last few years I had endured and wondered, *why me? Why James?* I thought about Daniel and what an idiot I had been to have believed his lies. I thought about my entire life crumbling around me and became overwhelmed, convinced that no one loved me or would miss me when I was gone.

I persuaded myself that my children would be better off without me, and they would go on to have good lives for themselves.

As I sat alone in the silence, evaluating the state of my existence, I could not find a reason to live. My grief distorted my reality.

As I pondered what to do, I thought about the cliffs near my home and a roadway that led straight to the water. The easiest route to death was simply to drive there and not take my foot off the gas.

Between the fall and the frigid temperatures, I would probably be dead within minutes. It seemed like the best solution.

I put the car in drive and pulled onto the road. I headed toward the beach as my heart and mind shouted back and forth, arguing with each other.

Within minutes, my view changed from the asphalt road to a sparse view of trees, cliffs, and the waves crashing against the rugged mountainous terrain. As the waves slammed into the rocks, the sea water surged fifty feet into the air. From two hundred feet up, it looked violent and cold.

As the car moved in slow motion toward the cliffs, I began thinking about my mom, sister, father, husband, sons, and friends. For a moment, I felt guilty. Guilty for wanting to leave my life of misery, and guilty for failing God because I had been taught that suicide is a selfish act, and I was far from a selfish person.

My phone rang, startling me, and I slammed on the brakes. As I glanced at the dashboard, I noticed that it was Daniel. I shook my head in disbelief and debated whether to answer; I couldn't tolerate more of his lies. Desperately needing to talk to another human in that moment, I accepted the call.

"Hi honey, how are you? What are you doing?"

I choked back a sob. "I'm driving, trying to decide if I'm going home or going to kill myself."

He laughed. "Why would you kill yourself?"

"Daniel, you have no idea what I am going through, or the devastation you have caused me. I don't want to go on."

Hearing my voice and realizing the severity of the situation, he changed his tone.

"What about your boys? They need you, I know you love them. What about your mom and sister? Your friends?"

He paused and listened to me sob uncontrollably.

"Kate, don't do it! I'm not worth it. No one is worth your own life. I love you, stop this nonsense and go home. I don't want you to hurt yourself, I could never live with myself knowing I was the reason. Please stop crying and go home."

For an hour, we kept talking, as he pointed out the reasons that I had to live. He somehow managed to convince me to drive an inch at a time, until I reached my driveway and parked the car. He did not hang up until I was safely inside.

Sometimes that is all it takes; another person to keep you going, even when that person is the one who hurt you.

I went straight to the washroom to clean my face, wipe away my tears, and tidy my clothes. I did not want anyone to know the thoughts that had consumed me that evening. After several minutes, I regained my composure, put on a smile, and faced my family and responsibilities.

I never told anyone about that night or how close to death I came. I buried it, as I do with all things, in the depths of my heart and soul.

Despite the pain he had caused me, Daniel saved me that night. As reality set in, over the course of the next few days and weeks, I decided that he was right. I had plenty of reasons to live.

I realized that I had to stand on my own. I was tired of being unhappy, and I decided that enough was enough. I had to change and find myself again.

I took time off work to get away from everyone. My friend, Michelle, and her cousin were taking a trip to New York, and I was invited to join them. It had always been a dream of mine to visit New York City, and I agreed to accompany them.

I bought the tickets, airfare, and hotel for less than one thousand dollars. I was excited to go and thankful for the break in routine.

While packing my bag, I noticed something odd. Liam had placed a package of condoms in my suitcase with a note that said, "Have an enjoyable time, but use protection." Almost a quarter century with him and this is what he thought of me. I do not know why I was surprised.

The sad reality is that he never knew me. He had never taken the time to get to know me, my heart and soul, who I am and what I am about. He never realized the gem he had in me, which is why he behaved like he did.

When I arrived at the hotel, I threw out the condoms, sat alone in the dark, and cried for hours.

I felt the heaviness of every teardrop as it rolled down the softness of my skin, their weight wearing a path down my face. The pain poured from the tremors in my body and the gasps of my breath. It was cathartic.

The next morning, I woke, my resolve and determination rejuvenated. "You cannot sit here for the entire trip. Get moving!" I said to myself.

I went on sightseeing excursions, bus tours, saw the 9/11 museum, and attended a play. I met up with the girls, and we went shopping, to dinner shows and tried new foods in quaint restaurants. It was a slow, relaxing weekend, odd as that may seem for the bustling, heavily populated city.

I bought gifts for the boys and for Liam, and one special gift for myself. It was a mug from the 9/11 monument store, and it featured the survivor tree. It resonated with me; a reminder of those who survived that horrible, unforgettable day in 2001.

The pain had eased temporarily, though it was short lived. The trip was over; time to return home, back to reality.

When I arrived home, Liam told me that I was not allowed to discuss my trip. Any gifts I had bought were immediately put away and never used, except the survivor tree mug. It sits over my fireplace as a constant reminder that I can and will survive.

The time in New York offered healing, distance, and an opportunity to re-evaluate my thinking and focus. I decided that I would take steps to get better, to change myself, and to get on my feet.

The old me had died. All that was left of my heart and soul was ash, but with death comes rebirth, and the opportunity to create something new and beautiful.

Chapter 20

Encouragement

Every now and then you meet an extraordinary human being, someone who is pure and untarnished, full of life and love. Khloe is one of those people.

My first impression of Khloe was that she was a younger version of me, before my life had turned upside down. She had a vibrant personality, and she was energetic and full of optimism. She was pure innocence. She was an excellent communicator and completely trustworthy.

Although she may be unaware of it, she had an enormous impact on my life. As we worked together, I saw in her a glimpse of the young woman I used to be.

It was her positivity that helped me rise; her support that encouraged me to shed the past and embrace a newer, better version of myself. She acted as my catalyst for change, offering the gift of friendship I had been lacking, and she taught me to trust again. She had gumption and knew her worth. She earned respect because she respected herself.

Khloe made me realize that there was more life for me to live; I had not lost the keys to a great future, just misplaced them. As we chatted, she reminded me that it is never too late to start over, to go to school, learn, contribute, and make a difference.

She was determined and infectious in her belief that there was more waiting for me. She refused to let me give up my dreams. She is one of the few women I have met in my life who pushed me forward and upward.

She is an incredible human being who carried me when I had no one, lifting me up when she could have walked over me. If only all women could do this for each other.

Chapter 21

Clarity?

As a type 'A' personality, I was unable to accept failure and defeat, and continued to rationalize and create excuses to stay in my marriage.

One Friday night, a few months later, Liam and I were home, watching the movie *The Girl on the Train*. There were many scenes that made me stop and think about gaslighting, trauma bonding, and emotional abuse. Something in that movie reached the depths of me, shining a light into the darkness which had overtaken my soul.

Like the main character, I had normalized the not normal. I had been making excuses and covering up behavior that should have been called out, not excused. I thought about it for weeks, and finally realized that what I had was not love, it was control and manipulation.

I had been trying to convince myself to give my marriage another chance, to view our relationship from his vantage point, but it appeared there was nothing I could do right. It was obvious that he was unhappy, angry, and miserable. It was sad; in some ways, I felt responsible for his unhappiness, and thought that I had placed too many expectations on him, as I continued to deny my reality.

We had become caught up in daily living and so accustomed to the pressure that we had lost the happiness and joy in life. Nothing that either one of us did was right or acceptable. There was little love left, or at least that was how it seemed to me. It was more a case of daily routine, duty, and expectations, and whenever the pressure mounted, so did his anger.

We simply did not function as a family unit any more. There was no respect, understanding, patience, or tolerance between us. We were tired of bending and twisting; both of us wanting to be ourselves and neither of us knowing how to communicate our unhappiness to the other. We were going in different directions, each with a different map, neither checking to make sure that the other was following. We had different visions of the future and how our life was going to be.

We ceased communicating; well, I know that I did, that stopped some time ago. Regardless of the subject of discussion, he shut me down, complained about the words I said and the manner in which I said them, and told me I was wrong. I was never able to complete a thought, let alone a sentence, and after thousands of interruptions, I stopped. Stopped talking, stopped communicating, stopped expressing myself, stopped hoping, and stopped laughing.

In fact, it reached the point where I really did not have anything to say or discuss, because there was nothing left to talk about or fight for. Topics as simple as the weather would bring backlash.

Sometimes he preferred me quiet and contemplative. When life was good, I never had much to say – well, only the positive. He was not accustomed to me spouting negative comments, bringing forward issues that required change. It was very out of character, and he did not like it.

As I battled with and confronted my reality, two things were clear: my relationship was not normal, and the person I had evolved into after years of being in this relationship was a woman I did not know.

Chapter 22

Kate – The Enabler

En·a·ble *verb* **1. To give (someone or something) the authority or means to do something. "The evidence would enable us to arrive at firm conclusions." Similar: authorize, sanction, warrant, license, qualify, allow.**

That's me, I am an enabler. It is difficult to admit and say aloud, but it is true. My issues and problems up to this point are because I have enabled people to hurt me.

I enabled my mother to become controlling by not rebelling or establishing boundaries, when I should have taken control of my own life. I enabled my husband's gambling and drinking by not putting my foot down and saying "enough," and when he didn't, I should have walked away, knowing my value and worth, respecting myself enough to say, "you're not doing this to me." I enabled Edward to get the administrator's position because I did not call the selection committee and tell them that it was my work he was claiming as his. In the larger scheme, while the examples he used were insignificant, it is the principle that matters. I could have stopped it. Now, I must live with the consequences of my actions, and it is a bitter pill to swallow.

I don't hate them, and I am not mad at them; I am mad at myself. I am angry because I am dying inside. I am being eaten away by my inaction, which has allowed this to happen.

Everything I did, every decision I made, was out of love. I continually thought of the other person, putting myself in their shoes, to do what I would want them to do for me.

This is where being nice becomes a curse.

Life is about balance. Yes, it is good to be nice, but at some point, the nice gloves must come off and the boxing gloves must go on. You cannot continuously be pleasant and agreeable, no matter how much you want to be. I hate admitting it because I have always believed that the world needs more kind people, more love, and more compassion.

I hate to hurt people. I avoid it at all costs because it tears me up inside; it is abnormal how much it affects me. I feel so deeply.

I have learned, over time, pain is the best teacher. When you experience pain, you never forget it, or the lesson attached to it. It becomes embedded in your brain, in a way that being nice does not. I can be sweet and kind to a million people a day, but the person I kick in the guts is the one who remembers me. I do not know why life works like that.

Mom taught me to turn the other cheek, but her thinking was flawed. This did not apply to every circumstance. You could not be nice to everyone all the time; it allows people to think they can walk over you, when they cannot.

Jesus did not mean that you should allow everyone to walk over you, and he certainly was not a people pleaser. When people did not like or agree with his preaching, they walked away from him, but he did not change his boundaries or go chasing them, begging for them to come back. He offered them the choice of leaving or staying.

His intended meaning is do not seek vengeance on the one who hurts you. There is a stark difference. By asking us to turn the other cheek, Jesus is suggesting we ignore what we do not want, and instead focus on what we do want. It took ages for me to figure out and understand this concept.

There is a price to be paid for being nice, and I have paid it, many times. To quote one of my previous bosses, "Kate, no good deed goes unpunished." Perfectly accurate.

In 2015, when Amanda moved in, I thought everything would work itself out. I believed that I was teaching my sons to be kind and care for others. I would take her side in family arguments because I was trying to show her that she was not alone. I was imagining how she must have felt as a stranger in a strange home. I was not trying to isolate my son, but that was the result.

William thought I was choosing her over him, that I was encouraging her abuse of him, when I had no idea that it was happening. He learned that I did not follow up on my threats of throwing her out if she did not follow the rules; he was unable to understand that, in my world, you do not throw people away. You love them, heal them, and help them. They are human beings, not disposable assets.

William and I once had a close mother-son relationship. The choices I made when I tried to help Amanda built a wall between us, and it has never been the same since. I tried to explain to him many times what I was doing, but he was aloof and distant, and it caused me great distress.

The pain of losing my relationship with my son is the biggest price I have ever paid for my actions. I have tried to repair our relationship, but the trust we had is absent, and it devastates me. He avoids coming home, choosing to spend more time with his girlfriend, Sarah, and her family. He does not seem to listen to or value my opinion. But he is still my son, and I try my best to guide and love him.

I feel disrespected by my children in my own home. Being nice and enabling Liam's behaviors allowed the children to grow up thinking that it was permissible to disrespect me. Monkey see, monkey do. It is what they saw their father do, why should they behave any differently?

From what I can tell, they only see me as a cook and a cleaner, nothing more, making me feel belittled and unimportant. They do not understand how I feel because I never tell them, simply to keep the peace. In this case, silence is anything but golden.

William even called me out on my silence once, when Liam was yelling at me, "Mom, why aren't you saying anything?"

I could not answer. He would not understand the prolonged abuse I had endured, or my inability to voice my concerns or defend myself.

My heart breaks as I reflect on the mess I have made. I wanted my sons to grow up to be good men, but the choices I have made may affect that outcome.

William has started drinking alcohol and has tried marijuana. All the preaching and teaching I have done since he and James were infants has been in vain. Attempts to express my deep concern are shut down and muted.

When I asked Liam to speak with him and offer guidance to steer him on the right path, he told me that William was old enough to make his own decisions and I should stay out of it. I cannot do that. I am his mother and I love him, and his future is too valuable to be ignored.

My only option is to continue to preach, steer, pray, and hope that some of what I say sinks into his psyche.

I have done my best to teach my sons about life, bringing them to church, helping with their homework, and teaching them how to study. I have encouraged their development by allowing them to make their own decisions, mentoring, and counselling them. But Liam often overrides my decisions and has not allowed me to teach them my values as well as his own. There are no words to describe how much it bothers me.

I often felt like I was raising three children. I had no one to lean on, discuss issues with, or seek guidance from. In many aspects of my marriage, I felt hopelessly alone and overwhelmed.

At work, I avoided confrontation with staff, resulting in the loss of good people; the ones who stayed should have been the ones to move on. The work environment was toxic and needed to be repaired. I have consulted conflict management specialists, and I have had to put on my boxing gloves. I hate it. I want people to come to work, do their job, and go home. Why is this so difficult?

It does not pay to be nice or enable others. Admitting it is a flaw in my character is the first step toward healing. I need to take steps to re-establish my boundaries. I need to take back my power, voice, value, and worth.

Chapter 23

"I Love You"

Those three little words can be life changing. As a young woman, I longed to hear them from a man who genuinely loved me, and I longed to say them to a man I genuinely loved. I cannot even begin to count the number of times I have had men tell me they "love me."

"I love you"…

as a friend…

and then walk out the door…

date someone else…

degrade me.

"I love you"… but… I need to work on myself…

you are overweight and I like slim girls…

I am a con artist.

It was never love, not by my standards or understanding of the word. A person who loves you will never hurt you, they will only want the best for you. They will support and defend you; they will help you grow and succeed. A person who loves you will never let you down; at least, not intentionally.

To be honest, those three little words mean absolutely nothing to me without proof that there is actual meaning and feeling behind them. You can tell me you love me a million times a day, but without attention, affection, and action, I won't believe you; time and experience have taught me not to.

I wonder if people really understand what they are saying when they say they love someone.

For me, it means I am staying by your side; I will protect you from all harm; we will have good days and bad days, but we will get through them together. It means lean on me, and I will lean on you. It is offering support, caring, sympathy, empathy, working together every day, and not giving up on each other.

I do not want to hear those words any more, unless it is from a man who is willing to support them with action; I have no time or interest in anything else. I long for the day when I can hear them and say them with conviction and meaning.

Chapter 24

Meeting Connor

Incredibly, I continued to talk to Daniel. A few months after the suicide episode, he began calling unexpectedly – asking how I was, if I was happy, and apologizing for what he had done. I decided to talk to him because I had to know why. Why did he con people? How could he live with himself to inflict such pain on another person?

I learned that he was from Nigeria and while it has a vibrant popular culture, there are ninety-five million people living in extreme poverty; people are starving, and many live on less than three dollars a day. Who could survive on such a miniscule income? Certainly not me.

Daniel was hungry and desperate. He needed me to fall in love with him so he could later ask for money, money that he needed to buy food to stay alive. My compassionate heart felt such empathy for him. I wished I could help him, and the thousands more just like him. No one deserves to live in such a manner.

Unfortunately, I was not blessed with a ton of money, and I was barely able to make ends meet myself. The only thing I could offer was my empathy, sympathy, and love, which is what I gave him.

I wanted to see what he looked like, and how old he was. Surely, he had to at least be my age, given the way he romanced me and the way we communicated. He shared a picture, but I was wrong again. He was handsome, but just a kid, twenty-five at most, and wise far beyond his youth.

I was so gullible and naïve. I could not come to terms with the fact that I had been played and he had taken advantage of my kindness. My heart is usually so guarded, I never let that happen.

Kate, you must let go, I told myself. The fantasy I had believed in was dead; my heart would never heal if I clung to an illusion that could never become reality. I deleted my email, changed my phone number, my Instagram account, and any way he could contact me. I had to move on.

I remained on social media. It was a mindless activity to occupy my time while my brain processed the thousands of interactions from the past few years. The messages kept coming – at least one a day, every day.

Martin messaged me on a Saturday morning while I was cleaning the house. I responded while in between chores, not wanting to be rude. He stated he was a geologist, and a divorced dad of a beautiful young girl. My initial response was, *here we go again*. My radar was on high alert, and I was highly suspicious of any stranger who was trying to interact.

We chatted and I explained how James' illness, and the chaos of 2016, had impacted me. I also explained the relationship with Daniel. He was sympathetic, kind, and a good listener. He empathized with me, but I could sense something was not right. I watched the language structure of each text, and the way he spoke when we chatted. It was all too familiar.

Once he refused to FaceTime or talk via video, I knew he was a con too, and I confronted him. He told me I was mistaken, but I knew I was not. We continued to chat, and I played along.

When he fabricated an elaborate story saying he was coming

to visit, I laughed to myself.

The night before he was supposed to arrive, we discussed plans for the next day. I waited to receive messages indicating that he was on his way, anticipating a text or two if he was truly travelling through different airports from one location to the other. But he did not arrive, and of course, I did not get any text messages.

He waited a couple of days before reaching out to me. When he did, he created a fake story to explain why he could not come, but I already knew – he was not who he was portraying himself to be.

I continued to press him for the truth, and finally, he confessed. "I am not Martin. My name is Mona."

He was thirty-one years old, single, from Nigeria, and he, too, was starving. Though he did not want to be defrauding women, he needed the money to survive. He shared a picture of himself in a blue dashiki. He was handsome and healthy, but very thin.

I prayed and asked God what to do. I assumed that I had to do something because he kept sending these men to me.

During prayer, I remembered that there was money left in an old savings account, and despite my own struggles, I withdrew it and sent it to Mona. I am not the kind of person who can sit down to eat knowing that someone is starving to death. He was very appreciative.

He had recently lost his mom, his dad was ill, and he was desperate. He was educated but unable to find a job or have gainful employment. He explained the challenges of working in Nigeria and that, to survive, many people had to defraud others.

I still chat with Mona, even to this day, and I have met some of his family via FaceTime. I need to know he is okay. He has become a friend. He needed love and support, and I gave it.

Most of my friends told me that I was stupid. "He is a con artist," they reminded me repeatedly. "How do you know what he is telling you is the truth?"

I don't, but here is the catch: God told us to love each other. He did not say only love the good people, the poor people, the church people, or the rich people. He wanted us to love each other (1 Peter 4:8: "Above all, love each other deeply, because love covers over a multitude of sins.") Love the sinners – and we are all sinners.

I do my best to love people and help them. If they are being evil or doing evil that is between them and God. I am in no position to judge anyone. I can only look after my own soul and do what I feel is the right thing to do. Nothing else matters, because no one else has walked in my shoes, done what I have done, or faced what I have faced. At the end of my life, when I go to meet my maker, I will tell Him that I did what I could. I loved everyone sincerely, with all my heart. I tried my best, and at the end of the day, I can live with that.

While talking to Mona, he mentioned a site called MeetMe. I assumed it was another social media platform he was using to meet and defraud women. Being curious, I went to investigate, signed up, and discovered that it was a dating app. Out of nosiness, I uploaded my photo. Within seconds, the messages came fast and furious. At one point, there were so many that the app crashed; a popup screen appeared, "please come back later – too many requests." I was shocked and giggled, "Well, this is new."

I received messages from men ranging in age from eighteen to seventy. As I looked through the hundreds of profiles, I responded to messages from two. One slightly older than me, one slightly younger.

I explained that I could not stay on the app because I was being bombarded with requests. If they wanted to talk, they would have to come find me on Instagram.

That is how I met Connor.

Connor, a graphic artist, was a handsome Irishman, in his late fifties, with gray hair, glasses, and a sweet smile. He looked innocent enough with pictures of himself, his animals, and his camper. Maybe he was real, though I was very doubtful. My trust level was at an all-time low.

We exchanged pleasantries, demographics, work history, and relationship status. He was very charming and piqued my interest. There was something familiar about him, and I felt an instant connection to him. He was endearing and appeared to be real, honest, and forthright. *Hmmm. Do I dare to hope?*

We chatted for several hours, the discussion lively and upbeat, as we discussed my European background and familial connections. There was an incredible sense of familiarity, as if I had met him somewhere before.

We understood each other perfectly; we *got* each other. We reluctantly departed for the evening, and when I woke to a video message, I was flabbergasted.

The message was simple and beautiful. "Hi Kate! I wanted to send you a wee video to let you know I am real." My mind was blown! He was not afraid for me to see him. He wanted me to trust him, and he was obviously curious about me. Checkmark: he was real.

We chatted frequently throughout the day, and I enjoyed our conversations. He requested we chat on FaceTime. Reluctantly, I obliged. As we chatted, we discovered that we shared many common interests.

Connor fell in love with me at first sight. "To me, you are the most beautiful woman in the world," he told me.

We were barely communicating for a week when he offered to send me a ring to prove his love. I was in shock; it was all happening so fast. "Now hold on, I'm not there yet!" I said.

He was adamant. The ring arrived a few weeks later from Dublin, by special guarded delivery. It was a beautiful fourteen karat gold wedding band, with "*Mo Anam Cara*" (my soulmate) etched in the band, engraved with Connor & Kate. *Wow!* Oh, my heart. I was sincerely touched, and completely overwhelmed.

Connor had been searching tirelessly for the person who would satisfy his intellectual desires and deep-rooted passions. During our initial interaction, I remember him saying to me, "Be careful, you may fall in love."

I chuckled and thought to myself, *There is no chance of that happening, given what I have been through!*

The irony lies in the fact that he never, not even for even a split second, believed it could happen to him. He had been searching for years and he had given up hope of ever finding what he craved and desired, coming to terms with the reality that it did not exist. There was no woman who could measure up to his standards, be his intellectual equal, or satisfy his longings as a man.

Unlike mine, his marriage, while not fulfilling, was not abusive. According to Connor, he and Maeve did not have sex. Early in their marriage, the act of sex was for the procreation of children. When the children did not come, the sex stopped.

Maeve, his wife, was not withholding it on purpose. They just did not connect emotionally, spiritually, or intellectually; there was no chemistry. There had not been any since the day they were married.

Though they had both been virgins when they'd married, his expectations were high, his dreams and fantasies vivid.

According to Connor, hers were not even close to what he desired; if, in fact, she even had any. Being a man of honor, he stayed true to his commitment and made the marriage work for over thirty years.

He would drown himself in his work to make up for his humdrum relationship, and he excelled in his profession. Maeve was a dutiful and responsible wife, keeping a lovely home, cooking, cleaning, and performing the tasks required of any homemaker, and they maintained a wonderful friendship.

As time passed, our love and sense of closeness grew. It was the first relationship I ever had that was built on a foundation of trust and honesty, and yes, I know that sounds ironic given we were both having an emotional affair.

We laid everything out at the beginning of our relationship – past, present, expectations, and where we were in our marriages. There were no secrets or lies. There was nothing to hide, and the foundation of openness and sincerity was laid.

At last, I had something to work with. God, it felt so good to have this kind of love, the kind that I had searched for my entire life.

I have often asked Connor what he thinks of me, and he describes me this way:

"You are a very remarkable woman, darling. You have the most amazing blend of beautiful qualities. You are strong at the same time as being weak, sophisticated even as you are beautifully simple. You can be leaned on even though you need to lean. You are magnetic, intelligent, romantic, sweet-natured, balanced, and never predictable. You are so easily touched and so readily felt. Loving you is so easy because you are so lovable."

And his opinion of me has not changed since the day we met. Incredible, I know; it is such a stark contrast to the way Liam views me. The difference is staggering.

Connor affects me deeply; it is difficult to express the

emotions he evokes. I am filled to the brim with fear, doubt, and insecurities. Connor somehow crawls inside my heart and soul, gently massaging salve on the wounds, healing them one at a time. The first time he touched them, I cried. But the next time was not as painful, nor the many times that followed.

He never, ever hurts me. He heals me in ways I never knew I needed, with love I never knew existed. He is the only man on the planet who knows the real me and accepts me for who I am. His love is like mine; he is the yang to my yin. He understands the world of expectations and standards, and his life is very comparable to mine. We share a sense of emptiness and loneliness in our lives, and we have found the love needed to fill that chasm in each other. We heal each other at our core – not surface wounds with Band-Aids, but deep emotional scars with love and tenderness.

I love his blunt honesty (he does not sugar coat anything), and how truthful he is with me. It reassures me that I know where I stand with him; there is no guess work or interpretation. It feels good not having to decipher his actions and thoughts. He says what he means, and he means what he says; I need that.

When we are together, I feel whole. He calms the storm that rages inside me with words of comfort and protects me with a shield of love. He does not care about how I look or what size I am, because he did not fall in love with the packaging, he fell in love with my soul.

Meeting him changed me, and as he invested significant time into the relationship, matching my effort, I knew he was sincere.

The trust we created, combined with his sincerity, knocked down the walls I had erected around my heart, and his love became the bridge over the moat that brought him home.

For the first time in my life, I had someone I could lean on and trust. I had a man who loved me for who I was without wanting anything but love in return.

For the first time in over forty years, I felt I wasn't alone. The little girl inside me was so relieved to take off her armor that I collapsed into the safety of his loving words.

As he wrapped his love around me, I released the pain I had been holding on to, and I let myself feel the losses I had suffered.

Having lived with and become accustomed to unfulfilled and empty promises, I was completely gob smacked.

He soothes me, reminding me daily of his love, reassuring me that it is real. He sends me money so I can have self-care time. He reviews my work and provides feedback. He listens to me cry and whine and offers me a pick-me-up, and he never asks for anything in return other than my presence and conversation; there are no strings attached. He is patient and kind, loving and supportive, strong, masculine, and intelligent, and he has the most fabulous sense of humor.

The emotional intimacy we share is rare. It far exceeds any preconceptions I had. He knows *me* – what I think, how I feel, the battles that go on inside my head. I often think, he knows me better than I know myself. When we are together, Connor is present, there are no competing priorities, because I am the priority.

We share respect, attention, and love; we listen to each other, without judgement or interruption. We share life, in the only manner we can. He compliments my mind, my looks, and my talents, understanding the many parts that constitute my whole being.

I wear the *Mo Anam Cara* ring on my wedding finger every day as a reminder that I am loved. I know that is surprising, and for some offensive, given I am married to someone else, but I feel married to him. I share a connection with him that I do not have with my husband.

He is consistent, dependable, and he stabilizes me by supporting me and letting me grow into the woman I was meant to be. I do not feel like I am on a wild roller-coaster ride with him. Our relationship ebbs and flows with the normal humps and bumps of daily life. It is the best feeling in the world. For those who have this – count your blessings, it is a gift.

There are just a few hiccups, like his wife and my husband – oh yes, and a few thousand miles – stopping us from being together. Like everything else in my life, it is more complicated.

Connor is a man of duty and honor. He has made a commitment to his marriage, his family, himself, and God, and he will not violate it.

It does not matter how much he loves me, or I love him, we will never be together. Heartbreaking, but true. Or at least that is where it sits right now. As each day passes, it is increasingly difficult to be away from him and apart from each other.

I passionately believe that he is my soulmate. There is no other reasonable explanation. In our fifty plus years of life, neither of us has ever had this type of connection with another person. That must account for something.

It is the kind of relationship you read about in books and shake your head, thinking *oh sure, like that exists*. It does, I have it. Well, sort of.

I have parts of that love, even if I cannot have the whole package. Given my circumstances, I will accept any version of normal that is given to me. I long for the stability that such a love provides, even if the future is uncertain right now. My friend says we are the love story yet unwritten. Time will tell.

Chapter 25

Dreams and Fantasies

Throughout my life, I have had many dreams of the future and what it would hold for me. We all have them, yet all are different. It is what keeps us moving forward. Some dreams go unfulfilled, but there is nothing preventing us from envisioning a new dream.

My dreams have been diverse. I dreamt of being a model – tall, thin, beautiful – the envy of women and the desire of men. Of being a mother – deeply loved by her children and sharing the enormous love that dwells deep inside me. Of being a boss – to be able to give people the opportunity to advance and help them move forward.

I dreamt of being a wife – married to a man who loves me and who would never leave or forsake me, knowing the love of a man who would protect me from harm at all costs. I have dreamt of my son made whole and the miracle needed from God to make that happen. I dream of bright and happy futures for my children.

Lately, my dreams and fantasies have been about Connor, the steps needed for a future together, and our first meeting. My imagination runs rampant as I dream of being held, loved, and kissed by him.

Connor and I have often chatted about our vision of the events leading up to our in-person meeting: a location familiar to both of us, utilizing a campervan to travel together and get to know each other. I have played it out multiple times, in a thousand scenarios, in my mind.

We would travel across Europe, to a variety of towns and places where we could be alone and explore our relationship. We would see if the months of online chemistry, longing, and anticipation were real.

This dream consumes me day and night; the possibility of a future with the man I love. It makes it difficult to focus and concentrate, and it intensifies the longing and yearning to be together. It leaves my mind filled with thoughts, questions, and possibilities to find the path to the one that my heart desires.

As much as I would love for this dream to become a reality, there is no obvious path to achieve it. Perhaps God is not going to answer my prayer. Maybe it is true – *what God has put together let no man put asunder*.

Is that God's plan for me – to love but never be loved the same way in return, to simply love from afar?

I love Connor, but he is thousands of miles away. I loved Liam, but the emotional abuse was more than I could bear, and though we live in the same household, our hearts and souls are worlds apart. I love Amanda as my daughter, but she will never be my flesh and blood. I love my children dearly, but they are grown and have a life of their own, and do not really need me.

The emptiness and loneliness equate to more time at home, alone, with Liam, while he watches sports, works in the garage, or does work for others. I am constantly lonely and alone, and I do not like it.

There is no money to go out or do anything, our financial challenges prevent that from happening. I just work, cook, clean, and sleep. Even though there have been small improvements, I barely have enough money to pay bills, and there is hardly any money left for the food required to control my blood pressure and diabetes.

Despite the challenges, I put on a smile and keep going because I am a survivor. I do not know how to quit, and I am too stubborn to give up. I expect I will die working, like other members of my family. It is not only in our blood, but in our genes too.

I carry these challenges and regrets with me every single day. My doubts, insecurities, and lack of confidence stem from the life I have lived and the choices I have made.

I was once strong and beautiful and thought I had the world by the tail, but if you get belittled and degraded often enough, you start to believe that you are not worthy. And when life keeps throwing up roadblocks that keep you from your dreams, you start to believe you do not deserve them anyway. You absorb the negative energy into you, and it becomes part of you; it is a part I do not want.

The insecurities that exist in me exist in all women, in one form or another. We are trained from birth to compete in a game that we cannot win, and we exhaust ourselves trying – to be the best mother, wife, boss; to be the most beautiful, to have the best body, to defy the natural aging process, attempting to stay young forever – it is an impossible task. As women, we need to know our worth and seek validation internally, not externally, because external validation is rarely forthcoming. We are worthy, even if no one on the face of the earth sees it, because God sees it. He made us, and we are beautiful.

I must learn to believe in myself again. There is a new version of me that is begging to be set free. I must unlock the gates of the cage and let her fly.

Chapter 26

Change

The chaotic state of my life could not continue, and I realized this was God's way of saying "you *have* to change." Sometimes, He has no choice but to force us to take steps on a path that we should have found by ourselves. My friend, Carl English, author of 'Chasing a Dream: The Carl English Story, gave me good advice, "never doubt yourself, never stop chasing your dreams, and always believe the impossible." I began walking the road toward a new life and an improved version of myself.

Step one: change myself, fix my health.

I wanted to improve my self-worth, and I began a lifestyle change and exercise program. I joined a gym and gradually began to feel healthier and more positive. I placed a sign on my dresser mirror that read: "now or never, your choice."

I rose every morning at six a.m., without fail, and walked on the treadmill for ten minutes, increasing the time intervals until I was walking for up to sixty minutes. It was the best decision I had ever made. The activity changed my mind, my body, and my outlook on life.

I changed the food I ate, having oatmeal for breakfast, chicken salad for lunch, vegetables, fruit, and water all day long. Every chance I could, I moved – up and down stairs, walking the dog, going out to the mall with James and William – and I lost seventy-five pounds. It was the lowest weight I had been since my pregnancy with James, decades ago, and I felt good about myself.

Never underestimate the power of activity and the role it plays in your life. In my opinion, it is singlehandedly the most important thing you can do. Being active heals you, provides discipline, and restores faith in your ability to cope. It clears your mind and provides stamina for the marathon of life.

Step two: regain my confidence.

I returned to school and took courses to prepare for my master's degree. I studied day and night until I was accepted into the program of my dreams. After two years of challenging work, I will receive my degree.

Obtaining my masters was a goal I had wanted to accomplish in my thirties, but once I was married with children, I never granted time for myself. Setting this goal was a wonderful reminder that I am intelligent and capable. I have a voice, and I want to share my thoughts with others, to let them know they are not alone or defeated. It empowered me and reminded me that it is never too late to grow and become a better version of yourself.

Step three: face my fears.

Whether I liked it or not, the day of reckoning was fast approaching. It was time to face the reality of my marriage and severe the bond of abuse, which had kept me captive. I deserved to receive the love I frequently gave to others.

The fear, which had played a dominant role in the negativity in my life, had to be replaced with a joyful, adventurous heart.

This was my biggest challenge. It is an uphill struggle to face your fears and harder still to change the way you have been programmed to think. It was time to think about my own basic needs and put them first – something that seems impossible when you haven't done it for so long, if ever. I also had to begin focusing on positive.

I never realized how negative I had become. It is astounding how many actions have changed me. How I have allowed the negativity in my head that says "you're not enough" to drown out my soul saying "you are enough. You can do it."

Step four: take time to heal.

I decided to practice positivity, work on my dreams, invest in myself, and be grateful for the gifts I have. This is where the true wealth and riches in life lie. There are no feelings in the world that can replace love or joy.

Music is the language of love, and I poured out my heartbreak, pain, and joy into a powerful music playlist designed to heal. I listened to the pounding drum beats, the wailing guitars, and the crescendo of the violins as they played each note with delicacy and empathy. In those moments, my soul exulted in the symphony of solace.

I decided to find pleasure in the simple things – moonlit skies, fragrant flowers, fresh snow, the warmth of the sun on my face – hoping that one day, my heart would be rewarded for its stubborn faithfulness.

I renewed friendships and relationships that I had left behind. I wanted to enjoy laughing, teasing, having fun, and learning to love life again. Life is not all gloom and doom; it only seems that way if you focus on it.

I began to re-establish my boundaries, and create new ones, so that I would never again give away so much of myself that I doubted my value and worth. I began to rebuild my confidence, knowing that I could fulfil my dreams if I just believed in myself.

That is the secret – *believe in yourself*, in your worth, your power, and your ability. Do not let anyone take that from you or try to diminish your light, your shine. It is a lesson I should have learned many years ago.

Chapter 27

Counselling

I am a strong woman surrounded by strong women, but even the strongest of women need help sometimes. They need to break down, cry, and heal the pain that they feel inside so they can keep going.

I was not afraid to ask for help, because I know that seeking help is a sign of strength, not weakness. My mind was not clear and had not been for so long that I did not know how I was ever going to function properly again. My emotions were confused, and the fog that surrounded me made me realize I was suffering from prolonged trauma. As I went about my daily routines, I could not decide if I were having a nervous breakdown, a midlife crisis, or just falling apart.

My employer offered a program where I could go for six counselling sessions at a time, and I readily accepted the opportunity. I am now in my third set of sessions, and I visit my counsellor once a month. I would not classify myself as being better, but I am recovering.

I am sorting through the mountain of emotions inside me and trying to organize them, so I can deal with them one at a time. I have a feeling that it is going to take a while – twenty years of abuse cannot be discussed in a couple of one-hour sessions with a therapist.

Describing the actions that transpired over the course of my marriage, which led me to this state of indecision and uncertainty, is not easy. For me, it's like trying to unravel the complexities of the universe. I struggle with what was love and what was abuse, what was controlled behavior and what was inadvertent. Naturally inquisitive, I must know why and how this happened so that it will never be repeated. Why did he manipulate and control me, and why did I tolerate it? The answers to such questions may never be found.

All human beings have a need for emotional support and communication. Having an emotional affair, to me, is in many ways worse than having a physical affair. The emotional bond that is created is exceedingly difficult to break. It does not wane as quickly as a physical relationship would, because physical relationships do not usually involve deep romantic feelings.

Knowing Liam as I do, despite his encouragement, he would never forgive my affair with Connor. In the early months of our marriage, he often replayed imagined scenes of me with other men in his mind and nearly drove himself mad– surely this would be no different.

Those were men he had never met, and I had never had sexual relationships with. I cannot imagine him suddenly understanding my reasons for needing support, or why I had no choice but to turn to someone else to satisfy my emotional and psychological needs. In his world, I have emasculated him, and I believe that he would never forgive me for it.

I had built an intimate relationship outside of my marriage for my psychological survival. I was starving for truth, honesty, attention, love, and companionship, needs that he could not provide, and I could not live without. I could not see any bridge that would connect these two worlds.

In essence, I made the decision to end my marriage by

having the affair, although I was not consciously aware of the decision for some time. Some part of me believed that the affair would be temporary and that, miraculously, life would go back to the way it used to be; the "happiness" I knew would return.

As time progressed, I realized that was never going to happen. Such events and indiscretions are not easily undone, and they frequently leave a path of destruction in their wake. Like most matters in my life, it became more complicated because I did not anticipate falling in love.

Counselling is complex, especially with an individual like me, who has multiple factors influencing my circumstances. My road to better mental health would be years in the making.

In the meantime, I surrounded myself with a healthy network of friends and family, people with similar interests and goals, and those who have survived similar circumstances. The adage is true, birds of a feather really do flock together. I cannot think of one of my friends, family members, or coworkers who is not going through something – whether that be abuse, marital difficulties, financial stressors, illness, suicidal ideations, or trauma. Fortunately, I have experience in all of them.

They come to me as a resource, as a survivor, to seek help in coping with the challenges they face. Many have commented that they feel better after having visited and chatted with me because I do not judge them. I offer compassion and understanding and hope for tomorrow. I assure them that no matter what their circumstances are, it will get better. The sun comes after the rain, and I believe that to always be true. No matter how long it takes, it will come.

My counsellor suggested that I write my thoughts as a coping strategy. I had never done so before, and I wondered if it would be effective.

I discovered that, as I wrote my truth and shared my pain, the roar of anger, hurt and pessimism raging inside me became quiet and still. It was in those moments that the healing began, validated by words on a page that I could not bear to speak aloud. The words and tears of my catharsis taking shape, creating a life of their own.

Chapter 28

Psychics

I am a strange bird, yes, I am. I believe in God, and I have faith that Jesus is my savior, but I am a sinner.

Healing, for me, comes from many sources, and I never look at it as being isolated in counselling. No sole source can cure all that ails you. I have always had a fascination with the unknown, and though it may seem odd, I sought advice from the strangest of resources – psychics. Unlike some Christians who think of psychics and mystics as tools of the devil, I visited psychics – initially as a laugh, and eventually because a lot of the card readings came true. I was intrigued.

I often visited the same psychic, Susan. She was frequently utilized by the police in Canada, the United States, and around the world, to solve many cold cases. She was particularly good, and gifted; a prophet, if you will. She told me of events that no one could know, and outlined future events which came true, so I bought into it.

Over the course of thirty years, I visited Susan for readings at least once a year. I was never a patient person and I always wanted to know what was coming and when. I do not mean that I ran my life according to the tarot cards, but I was curious about what the future had in store for me.

Having your cards read can be an intimidating experience, depending on the environment. Susan saw her clients individually, in a small office-like room covered in mahogany wood paneling. As I recall, there was one small window on the wall adjacent to the table, which was draped with black-out curtains, and a reading light that shone on the center table where she lay the cards. We sat opposite each other and chatted while she smoked a cigarette, sizing me up to get a feel for my personality as she prepared for the reading.

As I looked around the room, I noticed intricate – and eerie – sketches hung on the walls of people who had passed on, all drawn by Susan. She would encourage her clients to review the wall of faces as they arrived, hoping they may recognize someone. If they did, she would relay a message she had received from beyond the grave. Fortunately, I never recognized anyone; that would have freaked me out.

There were crystals and glass balls on a separate table, books stacked neatly on a bookcase, and the room was cloaked in darkness.

She was a different looking woman, with medium-length red hair, high cheek bones, deep eyes, and full lips, and she always wore red lipstick. Her voice was unique and, while she tried to sound soothing, it often unnerved me.

As we sat across from each other, she would begin the session by reading my palms, commenting on my lifeline, marriage, and children. Sometimes, she would ask for my rings to get a "better feel."

There would be two decks of cards – one to discuss the immediate past and the next three to six months, the other would involve the next three to five years. I always had to make a wish before we started, and if I had any questions on my mind, I would ask them quietly to myself as I shuffled the cards.

My questions, of course, revolved around love, marriage,

and finances. I was never overly concerned with employment because I was blessed to have a permanent job.

When I finished shuffling the cards, she laid them out on the table and explained each card as she turned it over, one by one. On the occasions when there was little going on in my life, half the table would be full before she could tell me anything.

At one reading in particular, my friend Ella accompanied me. When I walked into the house, I could sense the most negative, evil presence, and it felt like it was right next to me. It caused the hairs on the back of my neck to stand at attention and my pulse to quicken as the adrenaline rushed through my body, causing me to shift constantly in a state of uneasiness.

The psychic often looked past me, over my shoulder, during this reading, saying, "You are surrounded by three angels at all times." I do not know if she said this to make me feel better or to let the evil presence know that they could not get to me; either way, it was spine-chilling.

When Ella and I returned to our vehicles at the end of the reading, I told her about the evil spirit I had felt, and I decided that I was never going back. Having spooked her, she said the same thing.

Years later, we decided to try it again. The house had significantly changed; there were now holy pictures and statues everywhere – inside, outside, by the door, on the walls, and on the tables. The room in which Susan traditionally did her readings was closed off and boarded up. A rug draped over the door. It was eerie, smelly, and weird.

There were cats of every kind roaming throughout the house; their food, litter, and scent scattered over two or three rooms. Susan was doing readings in the dining room, where it was bright and full of natural light. As we laid out the cards, Daniel was everywhere in my reading, in every aspect of my life.

"He is not being honest with you. He is lying to you and there is something going on with him," she said.

She was right, he was a con, as I later learned.

As she reviewed the cards, trying to figure out his secret, time went so quickly that Ella did not get her reading done. Susan asked her to return the next evening.

Before they began, Susan took a silver necklace off her neck and gave it to Ella. It was decorated with holy medals of the Virgin Mary and St. Michael. "Give this to your friend and tell her to wear it constantly," she told Ella. "Can you please have her call me? I need to see her again."

I attempted to visit her three times, but each time she refused or was unable to see me. Instead, I resorted to visiting other psychics, hoping one of them could warn me of whatever danger surrounded me, but they could not. To this day, the message remains a mystery and I remain disturbed by it.

The odd thing is that no matter how many different fortune tellers or psychics I went to, all the readings were the same: my marriage was over, I would meet someone new, I would remarry, and I was destined for happiness.

I hope they were right. Honestly, I am still confused about my marriage. Meeting Connor and understanding his dedication and devotion to God, I wonder if I should try to be faithful and stay committed to my marriage.

Connor says that it is my decision and follows with "Kate, God won't be mad if you leave. Abuse is one of the reasons he will forgive you."

I am inclined to believe him. As a woman of faith, I cannot and do not believe that this life of sadness and misery is the life He wants for me. God wants me to turn to Him in times of trouble and lean on Him. It is He who will take away my pain, offer comfort, and support me. God loves me, God loves all of us. It does not matter our religion, race, color, or disability, He loves every one of us. Surely, He wants me to be happy, because by being happy, I will be better able to do His work.

Chapter 29

Guilt and Fear

I do not feel guilty about what I am doing or what I have done. Why? I have asked myself that question at least a thousand times, and the answer is, I do not know why.

Early in our marriage, when love was new, I would feel guilty for even glancing at another man. I would rarely act in any manner that violated my Catholic upbringing; my conscience was good and healthy. But as time passed and I lost increasingly more of myself, any guilt I had left with those pieces of me. Fear of his reaction dominated my mind and heavily influenced my behavior, preventing me from taking the steps necessary to confront my circumstances.

I do not want to make it sound like over time I became entitled to cheat, because I don't believe that. I do not think that cheating is right under any circumstances. Yet here I am.

Truthfully, I cannot fathom how I am allowing this relationship to continue, or how I allowed it to begin in the first place.

I despise cheating. Over my life, I would often proclaim that I would never participate in such two-timing activities. I sat on my high horse, explicitly judging those who cheated, stating how cruel it was, condemning such a selfish and unnecessary act. What a hypocrite I am.

I am the product of a family torn apart by cheating.

Considering this, you would assume that I would never allow myself to cheat, but that is not the case. Despite the effects it had on my sister and me, it was my mother's love that got us through the separation and divorce.

It helps to explain why I am like this. I inherited her loving, giving nature – I watched it, lived it, embraced it, and loved her for it. She wanted to love away any pain we had, removing it completely from our lives, and she did everything in her power to make sure that we did not experience those negative emotional effects.

You would think, given everything I have said about hurting people, that I would not want to hurt my husband, and I don't. I sincerely do not want to hurt him.

Why am I being unfaithful?

I cannot explain it. Maybe I think I am not hurting him, that he has no feelings. He did tell me to have an affair, after all.

Maybe I feel that he honestly doesn't care, and realistically, he has never been in love with me. I believe he was never interested in me as a person; he was only ever interested in the life I could give him, a life that he could never have had on his own.

After everything I have been through, there are days when I feel nothing at all – not guilt, love, sadness, or happiness. I am empty, numb… devoid of emotion.

He broke me; I am broken. As ridiculous as it sounds, there is something missing, some part of me I had and lost. Something I needed and, when it was not replaced or provided, I went looking for it, as if it were a basic human requirement, like that described in Maslow's hierarchy. You know, the pyramid of physiological and psychological needs, where each level represents a different human need, including food and water, safety, love and belonging, esteem and self-actualization. It is a model for understanding human behavior. As humans, we require those basic needs to survive; I am trying to survive and make myself whole.

We are all trying to collect those missing pieces that, at one time or another, we gave away and have never gotten back. We search for the missing pieces of our heart, mind, body, and soul, which should never have been given away in the first place, because we need them to be complete.

I do not have the answer to my struggle and journey. I try to reconcile what I was taught with how I feel, who I thought I was, and who I really am. I am confused about why I am going through this. Sometimes, I feel like I am a product of my environment, and sometimes I think I was made this way. It is the whole nature versus nurture question.

My drive to search is so strong that it must be innate, as if I were born with missing pieces and have been searching for them since birth. It is so odd, as if I were put here to find or do something, but I do not know what it is – a person, a place, a feeling? I am unsure, and I am frustrated because I cannot figure it out.

Chapter 30

Let Others Know They Are Not Alone

I honestly hate when people say that I am *too* nice. Is there any such thing? That single character trait has brought me both joy and grief. It has led to some of the best and worst decisions of my life. I struggle and wrestle with it every day, with every decision, wondering if it is going to help or hurt me.

I enjoy being kind and loving. Depending on the person and context, some make it sound like I am incompetent, or unable to deal with complex decisions, because they believe that empathetic people cannot be strong. They could not be more wrong. Believe me, I have no problem making tough decisions, my adult life has been full of them.

I find it even more interesting that no one ever bothers to ask why I am so nice. I think the answer might surprise them. I am this way because, after everything I have endured and survived, I could not imagine being any other way.

I have had more than my fair share of abuse, negativity, lost dreams, and lost hope in my life. I would never, ever want to inflict pain on someone like that which was inflicted on me. Sometimes the only joy I have in my life is to smile and have it reciprocated; to be kind and know the pleasure that it brings the other person. It brings me great happiness.

I believe that every person on the planet is struggling, which is why we must always be kind. You have no idea what a person is going through or how your simple act of kindness may impact their life.

For me, it is a method of overcoming the negative, overcompensating for the difficulties and bad decisions. It is my way of bringing joy, peace, and spreading love. It is the one trait I will never change.

I do not understand why people must be negative or hurtful toward another person. I cannot comprehend why they do not understand that we are all different, and each person brings something unique to the table to complete the picture. A one-of-a-kind puzzle piece, a piece to complement and bring fresh perspective, as described in 1 Corinthians 12: 4–31. (There are various kinds of gifts, but the same Spirit distributes them. There are diverse kinds of service, but the same Lord. There are various kinds of working, but in all of them and in everyone it is the same God at work. Now to each one the manifestation of the Spirit is given for the common good.)

Have you ever watched a person in pain? It is not pleasant, and it affects me profoundly. I remember one time attending the funeral of a young co-worker and meeting his father, who was utterly devastated. I looked in his eyes, and all I could see was his pain and the overwhelming sense of loss. For me, it was looking into the eyes of a tortured soul. As he held back his tears, I started to cry. As an empath, I felt his pain deeply. His grief filled me, and before I knew it, we were sobbing together.

I barely knew him or his son, but I easily recognized the pain he felt. I managed to sputter "I am sorry for your loss," before turning away. I could not bear it. I wanted to comfort him and wrap my arms around him and take away the pain and emotions he felt, but I did not know the man. Why would *anyone* want to inflict this kind of pain and grief on another, when we can barely stand it ourselves?

Many people – staff, friends, and others – have come to me with their problems and confided in me because they could not do so with anyone else. I give them my ear and a hug or two, a few words of wisdom and love to carry them through. It is my way of giving love, of doing what God tells me to do through His Holy Spirit.

I enjoy comforting people and the feeling that comes with it. I stepped into an elevator one day and faced a woman who was crying and clearly upset. The pain in her eyes was unmistakable. Without any hesitation, I walked up to her and gave her a hug. "I don't know what you're going through, but God wants me to tell you that it is going to be all right."

Amanda, with me at the time, watched in awe.

"Thank you for your kindness, you're very sweet," the woman replied.

"You're welcome. It will get better. Stay positive."

As we got off the elevator, Amanda asked, "Why did you do that?"

"I don't know, sweetheart; I just do what my heart tells me." It is the way I have been created.

Many people feel alone in this world, when in reality, all of us are struggling to get through another day. One of the greatest gifts you can give is to let others know that they are not alone. It is a beautiful offering of hope and love, and the world needs more of it.

Chapter 31

The Devastating Realization – 2020

Today was hell. It is 3.57 a.m. James and I went to see his new doctor. As an adult, it was time for him to leave the world of pediatrics and enter adult acute care. The only problem was that neither James nor I was ready for this change.

We registered, went through the screening processes, and were escorted into a small room with chipped yellow paint and posters of men's genitalia on the walls. There were two chairs and one examining table. It was a stark contrast to the examining rooms in pediatrics, which were filled with hope by way of children's characters and brightly painted walls.

There was no sugar-coating anything, no diplomacy in trying to convey a point, there were just facts; it felt cold. We discussed James' condition, his medications, and upcoming changes, as well as additional testing. I listened intently while James stared at the floor.

At four years into his disease, he was tired of being ill, and I could not blame him. I cannot even begin to imagine what he was thinking or feeling. He was a child when this happened to him, and he had been poked and prodded for years while they tried to determine the best course of treatment.

Today was the first time it sank in for him that this would be permanent; this was as far as he would progress, as much as he would recover. He tuned out the physician's discussion, responding only in quiet whispers when prompted. I answered the questions as best as I could. Everything was a blur, and the information was covered so quickly that I could barely absorb it all.

"Well, honey, what did you think of that appointment?" I asked when we returned to the car.

I laid my hand on his knee, as I had done many times before, as a sign of support. He brushed it away and stared out the window. I looked at him and my heart broke, a lump filling my throat. "Now, do not be like that. We will get through this."

In that moment, I could tell he felt defeated, and so did I.

I had promised him, when this had first happened, that I would make him better, that God would not let us down, and that "normal" would return with time, hard work, and patience.

He was not better, he was not normal, and I felt powerless and betrayed by God. I changed the topic as we drove home and attempted to cheer him up by treating him to an ice cream, but it didn't work. For the rest of the day and all evening, I could see his pain and his dejection, and it scared me into insomnia.

I do not like self-pity because I believe you should help yourself. I hate sickness because I do not know how to cope with it. I was shattered by James' response to the appointment, feeling completely depressed and helpless, because he had tried to help himself, but the outcome had not changed.

What is it with me and the universe? Why won't God answer my prayer and make my son whole? I cannot understand it. I try hard to be a positive person, to be hopeful and uplifting, strong and optimistic, but I feel totally betrayed and completely useless.

I am begging God to take it from him and give it to me. James does not deserve this; he is such a good boy. He is sweet, kind, honest, loving, and giving. He is a faithful servant. Save him and give it to me.

I cannot bear the pain as, once again, my heart is ripped from my chest and torn into a million pieces. I just want him to be normal again, to run and play again. Dear God, please hear my prayer!

Chapter 32

Struggles

I wish I could fix James and make him whole, heal my relationship with William, and take away all of Liam's insecurities, but these things are out of my control. All I can do is focus on healing myself and repairing the damage that the years of abuse and enabling have caused.

I struggle to portray how the relationship between Liam and I declined. Before I recognized the coercive control, it was the "little things" he ignored. I would spontaneously ask him to dance, go for a picnic, or dance in the rain, but the answer was always "no," or "I'm too busy," or "just stop it." The only thing that he was interested in was sex; it was the one thing he would never refuse.

I felt alone in many aspects of my marriage. Liam never attempted to make an emotional connection with me or make me feel worthy of his love. His lack of respect, attention, and love made me search for a way to have these needs met elsewhere.

I wanted a healthy relationship, where we could have fun, play together, romance together, share intimacy, share dreams, and solve problems; but what I had was a roommate. I needed Liam to listen to me and allow me to be vulnerable and open, but he built an impenetrable wall between us; one I could not scale. Over time, my inability to express how I felt whittled away at me, breaking me down piece by piece, changing me, and that changed my view of the world and everyone around me.

Listening to someone constantly question your past when you are trying to move forward, and having someone belittle and abuse you when you are trying to love them is exceptionally difficult.

I tried to be empathetic and sympathetic. I asked him numerous times to come to counselling to repair our relationship, but the answer was a firm "no." He did not consider talking to be a solution or a means of resolution. Instead, he believed that opening his heart and baring his soul would uncover more issues and lead to additional problems.

I tried to sit and discuss our issues rationally, but once he voiced his opinion, he would walk out of the room, leaving me unable to voice mine, completely shutting me down, and frustrating me. It left me angry and despondent. After he left, I would sit and stare at my phone, hoping and praying that somehow a solution would miraculously pop onto the screen.

I have learned that there is no point trying to build when you cannot agree on what you are building. I wanted to build a skyscraper; Liam wanted to blow it up. I wanted a strong, loving relationship, to build a home and a family; I wanted something majestic. Liam wanted to survive; that is all he knew how to do. He did not know how to thrive or build, and every time I would lay the foundation, he would tear it down. I eventually became so weary that I stopped trying.

I do not know if my love ever penetrated his heart. I know there was no soul or mind connection, at least not on my behalf.

I am such a romantic, tender person. I love sharing, communicating, touching, and being intimate. I love deep conversations and learning about each other, swimming in the limitless depths of the soul and mind, exploring thoughts and ideas.

To me, sex without love and intimacy is mechanical; it serves the purpose of procreation. You get on, you get off, end of story. But when you love someone and they love you, making love is a sharing of souls, minds, and bodies. It is the act of giving yourself to another person, a holy and sacred act. I think that many people have lost sight of the fact that it is a true gift.

Over the years, Liam would ask if he turned me on, and yes, of course he did. I loved him, he was a good-looking man with a great body, but sex without time for intimacy and connection wanes. I eventually lost the desire for sex because it had become mechanical, with no love involved. I mean *love*, not foreplay, a deep spiritual connection that makes you long to look into their eyes as you become one, a feeling of joining together to share something beautiful. Eventually, sex became solely for his sexual gratification, and I felt isolated and inconsequential.

Romance was non-existent. He seldom commented on my appearance outside of the bedroom. Comments like "oh, I love your big tits and round ass" are not romantic, they are derogatory and make a woman feel like an object for sexual pleasure. Women are so much more than sexual objects.

What is romantic, to me, is a man saying, "Let me follow your beautiful curves and adore your body, let me gaze into your eyes, and my desire be expressed in our kiss," as Connor did, or "you are my goddess." It's comments outside of the bedroom, which occur unexpectedly, like in the middle of the day when you are brushing your hair, or your teeth. It is appreciating my value and understanding what I bring to the relationship.

Romance can be shown by performing simple acts of love that demonstrate caring – putting a blanket on you when you are sleeping, calling to make sure you have arrived home safely, cooking something to eat, or encouraging you to go to bed and rest. It is bringing you flowers or calling to say hello unexpectedly in the middle of the day. The gestures do not need to be grand and elaborate. These little things keep a relationship alive and thriving.

The irony lies in the fact that Liam and I shared many of those unexpected moments; it is why I fell in love with him. But once we were married, the acts of kindness disappeared, and as a result, so did the intimacy.

Throughout our marriage, I made a point to kiss him good night every night and say "I love you" before falling asleep. One night, I decided to stop this routine, and I wondered how long it would take him to notice. It has been four years.

It is hard to feel connected and cherished when the little things are not noticed. It did not matter to him, but it mattered a lot to me.

I often asked him, "Do you love me?"

He always responded, "Yes, I love you," and continued with whatever it was he was doing. There was no stopping to come and kiss, hug, or hold, no providing reassurance. There was just a quick response to keep me quiet, making me feel like I was not worthy of his valuable time.

I would then follow up with "tell me." Meaning, tell me you love me. I hated that I had to ask, and I hated that it was frequently spoken in the bedroom, but not outside of it.

There was no lying on the couch together, no cuddling or snuggling, no back rubs or foot rubs. There was no time or interest for kissing or connection. Over time, we became friends with benefits.

Once that door closed for me, it stayed closed. I could not get it back no matter how hard I tried. The abuse, lack of communication, touch, and connection severed the link to romance and desire. For most women, mental connection is essential. I craved intimacy but never received it, and I eventually I sought it in other ways, by flirting, seeking attention, and hugging others.

Somewhere, somehow, I believe that he stopped loving me, although he may not realize it. Whether it was because we alienated each other or ourselves, or his insecurities became too much to deal with, I am not sure, but I'm convinced that he no longer loves me – if he ever did.

When he says "Kate, I love you," it sounds convincing, but I have grown to believe that he says this out of fear of letting go and losing his routine, not because there is real emotion behind it.

When I told him about Daniel and expressed my desire to leave, his response was not "oh my God, I cannot lose you. We will figure it out and find a way to make it work." His response was "oh, great. Now I will end up with some skank."

That one statement says it all, doesn't it? He was not thinking about me or our family; he was thinking about himself. He has had a single mindset for most of our marriage.

I am sure this may sound strange, but I do not know where to go from here; or if I do, I do not want to go there. It is tough to step outside my comfort zone and let go of something I have had for so long – or something I *thought* I had. Yet, the only way to grow is to face my fears and take that step.

The reality is that my marriage is over, and that kills me inside. It is such a bitter pill to swallow when I wanted to be different from my parents.

The question I must answer is, what am I going to do, and how and when am I going to do it?

My training in conflict management tells me to make an agreement with myself and start taking small steps. But what if I am too afraid to move?

I am struggling with everything these days, from words and actions to next steps. I cannot seem to bring myself to some sort of conclusion or resolution. I struggle with who I am and who I have become, the direction I am supposed to take, and the path I am supposed to choose.

If anyone had predicted that I would be having an emotional affair, I would have laughed heartily at such a ridiculous possibility, and then reminded that person that my upbringing would never allow it. I am a good woman, a faithful wife and servant. I love as Jesus taught me to love, and I try to do what is right.

I had been true to my vows and faithful to my husband in good times and in bad, fulfilling my commitment regardless of the circumstances. But what happens when your partner does not live up to your expectations? Are vows one-sided? I hear all the time that man's ways are not God's ways. God's rules transcend time, which is why you must be true to them, but it seems like an impossible task that is destined for failure.

Everything in my life feels so wrong. They say you must die to be reborn, and I believe that to be true, but it is the transition from death to life that I am struggling with. Who have I become? Do I want to be that person? Do I give up the only piece of happiness I have known, which is keeping me sane and alive?

Connor has shown me true love. He is sincere, his actions prove that daily. In my heart, I know that he deeply loves and cares for me. He lifts me up, making me a better person, and I do the same for him.

Liam wants me to be the negative person that he has created

in his mind. He tries to control and manipulate, bringing home junk food and encouraging me to eat it, discouraging me from going to the gym or getting my master's degree, saying it is cost prohibitive. Yet there is always money available for his weekly – often daily – alcohol and cigarette consumption.

He pushes me down even if he does not mean to, and although I sincerely believe that he is not doing it on purpose, he does not seem able to change his actions or mindset; it is automatic. It is killing our relationship and ruining any chance we may have for a positive, healthy future. Yet we took vows to love and honor each other, in good times and in bad.

Having been set in his ways for so long, is there any chance he would or could change? Part of me wants to believe he could, and part of me knows he won't, that he can't. He has not been wired that way. It makes me think of the quote "consider how hard it is to change yourself and you'll understand what little chance you have in trying to change others."

Do I stay or, according to my faith, damn myself to hell for eternity by choosing Connor?

My head hurts with the thoughts of the future and the past, what was and what will be. It hurts knowing that there is no way out without causing pain – for me, for him, for the kids and the family.

I do not know if I am strong enough to do it.

Chapter 33

Status Quo

Life is never a box with a big tidy bow or an arrow that aims straight. Despite my repeated attempts to move forward and follow my plan, I frequently fell back into the darkness I was trying to escape.

The status quo went on for a long time – years, in fact. You know the phase, where you pretend to the world that everything is fine, but in your heart, there is a category five hurricane. The external part of you, the part that everyone sees, is calm, cool, and collected. You say please and thank you to your spouse for the acts they do for you, and at the same time wonder how you can go on putting up a façade.

You look at your children and wonder how the dissolution of your marriage will impact them. When is the best time to leave? Should it be in the summer, giving them time to recuperate before school? Before Christmas, so they are happy and not focused on the separation, but on the joy of the season? It cannot happen at exam time; I would never want to impact their education and future.

The reality is that there is no suitable time. There is just time and what you are going to do with it. I could wait forever; I hate confrontation.

Every day I get older, not younger, and every day that I wait, I reduce the chances Liam and I have for happiness. I do not want him to be unhappy; I want him to find a love that satisfies his needs, just as I want a love that satisfies mine.

Every day the struggle grows, and I find it increasingly difficult to justify my actions; to condone having an emotional affair. Liam notices the change in my behavior and senses that something is wrong. He has not commented on the past in a long time and seems to be trying, in his way, to make improvements. Is it real change or fear? Knowing me as he does, he is afraid. When I make up my mind to do something, nothing can stop me.

The sarcasm and impertinence continue, but now it stems from hurt and frustration. He is so full of anger, and it saddens me. He cannot comprehend what has changed in me. My usual routine is to get mad, get over it, and move on, but I cannot seem to get past *this*, whatever *this* is.

Some days, I feel I am incapable of love, as if my heart has turned to stone, as if my soul has been vanquished. The landscape that I once knew no longer exists; it is radically transformed, like the damage from a hurricane.

I contemplate whether I should wear a ring on my finger at all; in my heart, my marriage is over, and Connor is never leaving his wife. I do not feel like I am committed to anyone.

I still have those moments where I recall the past and weep. Lying next to Liam in bed as he snores, whimpering to myself, "What a mess, what an absolute mess I've created!"

The echoes of Daniel's voice in my head, whispering "I love you, Kate," causing a cascade of emotions, pain, and devastation. *How could he do what he did to me? Did he ever love me, or was I truly just a pawn in his game?* I am not the type to be easily deceived, and I wanted desperately to believe that he really did love me.

My heart does not lie, it knows love. Connor loves me, and

there is an incredible and undeniable chemistry between us but continuing a relationship with a married man who has no intention of ever leaving his wife seems pointless. He simply cannot leave, because the stakes are too great and the devastation from the fallout would be too extreme.

Like me, he cannot afford any missteps. We do not have enough time left in life to recuperate if it does not work out. I get it, I understand it, yet I cannot let him go. He is my soulmate, my sanity, and in his world, I am his. There is no way for any of this to end well. We are setting ourselves up for more heartache and pain.

What are you doing, Kate? What are you waiting for?

I do not know.

Life is sometimes better in the status quo. You do not make any big decisions, pretending that everything is normal, and you go about your daily life without having to change a thing, but you are not living, you are existing. Is this what I want, and if yes, for how long? When will I end this madness and move on?

When I spoke with the psychic, she told me that one day I will wake up and everything will be clear. I wish that day would come, for it surely has not yet arrived. I am weary.

Chapter 34

Regrets

It is awful to live a life of regret. To be so dismayed at your decisions and to consider the hundreds, if not thousands, of different possible outcomes. To wonder how any single decision could have changed your path toward the direction and life that you always wanted. To want to change your life so completely that you want to be a different person, at a different time.

I do not know what is worse, regretting what you've done, or knowing that your life is more than half over and you have not accomplished even one third of the things you wanted to do. What's even worse is knowing that the likelihood of these things ever happening is slim to non-existent.

I struggled to come to terms with the realization that, after years of arduous work, there will be no funds for a secure retirement, no means to travel and see the world, and no way to financially secure my children's future. The romantic evenings of being alone with a loving partner, learning about each other and having meaningful conversations will never occur, and the closeness I craved will go unfulfilled.

To work and struggle your whole life in the hope of achieving a more prosperous future and giving so much of yourself and your energy to others without having received much in return is exhausting, and debilitating.

Though it frustrates me, we all make choices and then face

the consequences of those choices. While we cannot always control the outcomes of our decisions, we can control how we react to those consequences, and we can learn from them.

Regret is an opportunity to pause, reflect, refocus, and learn from the mistakes of the past. It is the time to take corrective action to improve your future by making better decisions. Like a mirror that turns inward, it shines a light on the person you are versus the person you are striving to be.

For me, regret has been a reminder to think carefully before deciding, and a way for me to determine who, and what, it is that I really want in my life.

The one thing I know for certain is that taking time to feel regret has also shown me that not everything can be fixed or undone. Some decisions can never be reversed, but life is meant to be a learning experience. It is not meant for you to carry your baggage with you twenty-four hours a day, seven days a week.

On our journeys, regret is an emotion that is not to be harbored but examined for its lessons and then released. My mom often paraphrased Maya Angelou saying, to know where you are going, you need to examine from where you came. Learn from your past and move forward.

The reality is that some people and things are not meant for you, no matter how much you wish they were. Some situations will not work out, no matter how much wishing, hoping, and praying that you do, and that is okay. No one has a life path that is perfect; we all move back and forth, up and down, succeeding in some areas and failing in others. Accepting that something is not meant for you is the first step forward. Letting go is the second. When you finally let go, the path you are meant to take will become clear.

Having been through so many devastating experiences and

decisions, if I were to give any kind of advice, it would be to follow your dreams. Listen to and follow the voice inside you that screams, "this will make you happy" or "follow this path." It is your soul speaking to you and believe me, it knows where you are supposed to go.

I know your parents are there to guide you, but they cannot live your life for you. It must be your life, your decisions, and your consequences. Listen to their guidance, apply the lessons they want to instill in you, walk to your destiny, and do not be afraid of failing. At least when you fail, you will know you have tried. Learn from your mistakes and try again.

I must carefully consider the path ahead of me. My next move is a big one. It can change everything.

Chapter 35

The Risk

I am the kind of person who must assess every angle of every scenario before deciding to do something. I like to have all the answers, to be prepared for what may come. It is time consuming, thought provoking, soul searching, and an explanation for why it is taking so long for me to act.

I must decide between staying and accepting the inevitable choice of leaving. I must be certain there is no way to salvage what I have. I hate being alone, I dread it, but that seems the path in front of me. I must go into survival mode, again – or maybe it is just an extension of the survival mode I am currently in. My God, it is mentally and emotionally draining.

When I reflect on my parents' separation, it was easier for them to come to the decision to separate because there was a clear violation of the marriage contract. I do not believe it is as simple for me. I suppose I do not see my infidelity as a violation because I have not crossed that boundary into physical intimacy.

A friend recently asked me, "What do you want?"

I laughed, "No one has ever asked me that question."

Sad but true, and scary, really.

"You know, it is only as complicated as you make it," he replied. Apparently, I have made it excessively complicated.

My counsellor says it's best to isolate the relationships and deal with them one at a time. She is right; being in love with one man while living with another does not make for a clear mind. It clouds emotions, thoughts, and does not help to rectify the problem.

How can I tell what I want if I am living a lie? That is a tough question, which provokes thoughts and more questions.

There is so much to consider: the relationship, finances, children, family, religious vows. I am struggling to sort it all out. For anyone who thinks it is a quick decision – it is, until you are the one having to make it. You must figure out where you are going to live, how it will affect your children, your job, your state of mind, and if it is worth the complete upheaval.

It is sad that I am not alone in feeling like this. I think about Daniel and Mona, and how incredibly unfair it is that there are people using the façade of love to cheat and lie; and women worldwide are so desperate for love that they are willing to pay for it by sharing and sacrificing their life savings to get it. What does this say about romance and the relationships between men and women?

I wonder if men understand that women want to be loved, appreciated, and given tenderness and kindness. We do not care about money. Well, yes, we all have a desire to be comfortable, but what matters is how you treat us, how you love us. We want your time, not your pocketbook; we want to know that you have our backs and will be our support in times of crisis. We want you to take your time and love us slowly, intimately, and passionately. We want your heart, soul, mind, and body, not a quick, meaningless romp in the sack.

Do men and women know the difference between love, lust, and infatuation? It appears we have forgotten how to love, and instead marry out of convenience; lusting after those we cannot have; infatuated by the idea of love with no understanding of what constitutes real love.

It appears, love is no longer sacred and precious. The desire for sex has replaced the desire for love; men expect women to give themselves freely for sexual gratification, and if they do not, they move on to someone who will.

It is time we re-evaluate what we are doing to ourselves and our relationships. It is time that women take back our power, to begin building each other up instead of tearing each other down, to start supporting and encouraging each other to lead better lives.

I think about Liam. Could he ever change, or has our love been lost with no chance for a future relationship? I think about the night we laid in bed together, when he whispered, "Do you know that what I've been doing to you is mental and emotional abuse?"

"Yes, I do."

He laid back and cried.

Was that a revelation, an acknowledgement of wrongdoing? Oddly enough, from that day on, he seemed more intent on stopping the name calling and the demeaning, demoralizing behavior. It made me wonder if he had sought counselling himself, and if he had begun his own road to recovery. I may never know the answer.

Is Connor my soulmate? Was our meeting meant to provide support and comfort to each other, to let us know that we are not alone? Was it meant to be more of a life lesson than a lifetime?

When I reflect on how we met, I am in awe. I honestly believe that our love and relationship was a gift from God, because if I were to calculate the odds of us meeting in the same place at the same time, it seems the only logical answer.

I find it fascinating how a series of moments can spark a meaningful story, as if God has a plan for your life, a predetermined destiny. The single threads of time coming together to create an unexpected tapestry of beauty, even if there are threads of a color you may not like. Somehow, each thread brings the right shade to the right place.

I think about our society and how we dispose of things so very easily. How we throw away some of the most important things in our lives with the belief that there is more out there – jobs, friendships, marriages, our elderly, respect for ourselves and our parents, and sometimes even other human beings.

I think about the cycle of abuse and violence; how most people experiencing coercive control think it is normal and a part of life, unaware that they are being manipulated. It is incredible how easily the cycle begins and repeats itself, and how it is unrecognizable when you are living in a constant state of anxiety.

I think about myself, who I was and who I have become, and I think about the ways in which life has shaped me. I reflect on the awful decisions I have made and how angry I become with myself for not being strong enough to stand up for what I want.

Sometimes, I feel like I am a child's toy bouncing around aimlessly in the water, bobbing up and down, searching for something but never knowing what I am looking for, with no shoreline to ground me.

The questions I asked myself when I was thirty, I still ask myself. So many thoughts and unanswered questions.

I need to spend time getting to know myself and seeing what others say they see in me. It is ironic that I do not see myself the way they do. For all the analysis and overthinking I do, I have never spent time trying to figure out what I want out of life. Pummeled by everyone's thoughts and expectations, I have had no time to reflect and figure out my own.

It is time that I learn to trust and respect myself, figure out what I offer and bring to life, and put myself first for a change.

At the end of the day, I love hard; it is an all or nothing kind of deal. It is deeply ingrained in the fabric of my being.

Finding the same kind of love in another person feels like an impossible task. To be honest, I have never met anyone who loves like I do. For a long time, I thought I was an anomaly, having been on this earth without the same kind of love for more than half a human lifetime. I have searched most of my life for it and have never found anything even remotely comparable, until recently.

Loving is not easy. It can give you the greatest highs and the lowest lows. Sharing your vulnerabilities with another person subjects you to the possibility of rejection and pain. Offering up your fragile heart is a risk, but it can bring the most beautiful of rewards, the greatest of joys, and the happiness we desperately seek. I believe it is worth the gamble.

Chapter 36

Scared 2020

As I tried to move in the direction of a new and improved me, fate continued to throw boulders in my path. Somehow, with the help of God and support of Connor, I hurtled over them.

There were moments of happiness interspersed with the madness, like when James received his driver's license. He was proud of his accomplishment, and I was happy for him. Life was not always cruel and unforgiving.

In January of 2020, I began my master's degree online. COVID-19 arrived in February, disrupting travel and daily life. I was overloaded with work and did not have time to focus on the past; there was barely enough time to deal with the present.

At my office, the other staff grew more uneasy and rebellious with the changes taking place, but I kept moving, protecting, guiding, and assisting. I offered comfort to everyone during the ensuing waves of panic.

Scheduled to graduate in June of 2020, COVID removed any chance of a normal high school graduation from James and the rest of the graduating class. We celebrated with family and friends, ate cake, and took pictures to capture the moment. It was far from ordinary, but we were delighted and proud to acknowledge his achievement.

Around the world, the incidence of COVID exploded, but I was undeterred from my new path, no matter how many challenges it brought. Fear was omnipresent. I was scared – terrified – of what the future had in store for me, but I was gaining strength and conviction with every step that I took, large or small. I was resolved to restore balance in my life.

Before the events of 2016, I had believed that I was in control of everything, but the events of that year, and every subsequent year, have taught me very clearly that God is in control, not me. I control absolutely nothing.

He has made me bow down to Him in humble reverence with the acts that He can perform and how He can change lives in an instant. A lesson I learned not once, but twice in the span of five years.

It is not that I did not believe in the power of God, but more a case of never witnessing it so powerfully.

In 2020, when the world stopped and one virus brought us to our knees, every bit of normal we knew disappeared. People lost jobs, homes, safety, and security; welcome to my world in 2016. Unnerving isn't it, to be shoved out of your comfort zone into an unfamiliar world?

Yet, I have survived, through the difficulties, depression, abuse, and complete turmoil in my life.

It has become obvious to me that I have a purpose, a role to fill. My life has meaning to this world, even if it is unknown to me. I have a gift to share, a unique piece to the puzzle that belongs somewhere in someone else's life. A distinctive gift that we each possess, and are encouraged to share, because no one else can fit where we do.

Armed with the belief that there is more for me, I continue walking my path, even if I am unsure of where it leads. I have the emotional support I need, even if it is thousands of miles away, and only God knows who else will be sent to guide and support me.

As COVID rages on, Connor worries about me, and I understand why; I am like a rag doll, pulled in every direction from pillar to post. Coupled with the trauma from the past few years, he wonders how I function.

I have no downtime, no time for relaxation or fun. I am at the disposal of an insane work schedule and hours of work I do for free. I tried to convince myself that it is better than going home, but it is not. I need to continue to put my trust where it belongs – in God. He will not fail me.

It is time to refrain from letting the outside forces of the world dictate my decisions. Listening to the noise of the world, while failing to listen to my own voice, has brought such chaos, unhappiness, and disorder. I must stop being concerned with what others say and think because I cannot control it, no matter what I say or do.

It is time to take another step – a baby step or a big step, it does not matter – but I must take a step. It is time for me to commit to myself, get out of my comfort zone, and accept the purpose for which I am destined.

People survive failed relationships every day, and they go on to make a better, happier life. No one said it would be easy; and if you cannot see the path, make one. I have always had that thought process – where there is a will there is a way. I can find the way. I am strong, no one can take that from me. I have God. If God is for us then who can be against us? The answer is no one.

Chapter 37

My Heart and Mind Are at War

The magnitude of ending a marriage is enormous. Leaving your spouse is a difficult decision to make. Never think for a minute that it comes without much thinking, meditation, and struggle. Personally speaking, it is one of the most painstaking processes that you could ever go through, even more so if you have a strong religious belief or faith, as is the case for both Connor and I.

After we met, it did not take long before Connor realized that he had found "the one," and he had no intention of letting me go. None. It is why he sent the 'Mo Anam Cara' ring within the first seven days. He wanted to solidify the relationship.

He knew long before I did that we were a match, and he never fails to tell me, every day since we met, how perfect we are for each other. I cannot disagree – we are, on many levels. We can finish each other's thoughts and sentences, and often laugh together when we do. The connection and the chemistry are so strong that they are palpable. There are times when it is as if we can feel each other, as if there were a presence. It is inexplicable and unfathomable, but it is *real*.

The more challenging question was how to move forward. Connor and I wanted to be together and out of our marriages, but never knowing if the chemistry would exist in person was a problem. Though we had no doubt that it would be vibrant and alive, circumstances were complicated. A single person only needs to think of themselves. A married person has so much more to think about. There are many commitments and responsibilities of significance.

It is easy to judge others who cheat when you sit on the outskirts of a relationship, unable to see the complexities that exist between the individuals involved. It is easy to judge when you do not feel the absence of love, the loneliness, or the emptiness in a relationship. When you go through it firsthand, the stakes are higher, and it is not as easy to make the decision that seems so obvious to those on the outside. Life can be complex, tangly, and messy.

Whether it is an emotional affair without sex or a physical affair, the sad reality is that no one has walked in the shoes of the cheater. No one knows what horror they have endured, what loss they have been through, or how much of themselves they have had to sacrifice to stay committed. No one knows but the person going through it.

Marriage is a lifelong commitment. As they say during the vows, it is not to be entered into lightly. "Marriage is not to be entered into unadvisedly or lightly, but reverently, deliberately, and in accordance with the purposes for which it was instituted by God." Powerful words to be heeded and understood *before* marriage.

Agreeing to be a person's spouse comes with an enduring and permanent commitment. For Connor and me, a vow was a serious, sacred promise for the duration of our lifetime. It was not a fly-by-night decision, but one made with conviction and a deliberate and profound belief of fulfilment. Neither of us considered, for even a moment, that these vows were unachievable, until life happened. I suppose that, on some level, our expectations of marriage were unrealistic.

I cannot begin to tell you the number of times we have prayed and questioned our vows. Or the number of times we have combed the Holy Bible together, looking and praying for guidance. It has been an enormous struggle.

In tumultuous times, you need your spouse to lean on; you need them to provide support, love, and patience. It is critically important that you know the person well before you enter marriage. You need to discover how you will face trials together in the future. A person who does not support you when you are single is not going to suddenly support you as a spouse, I promise you.

Raising children can be a nightmare if you do not agree on the values and beliefs to be shared with them. It can make life uncomfortable if one partner is unhappy, I am living proof of that.

The reality is that people are unfaithful because there is something missing, and that missing piece is different for every person. Something in the marriage is not making them whole, creating a void.

People attempt to fill the void in numerous ways: spending exuberantly, drinking, gambling. They hope that life will return to normal once they have had their "fix," and that they will once again feel whole. Some people call it a "mid-life crisis" or "finding themselves and their inner peace." Some people may do the honorable thing and address it with their spouse; while others fear hurting their spouse, believing that they would never understand.

The reality is that you will be unhappy until the void is filled with the pieces that were lost. It is the reason why marriages fail, and why people should seriously consider if the person they are with before marriage is *the* person they want to be with for the rest of their life. Just because you love them does not mean the answer is an automatic "yes." You need to seriously consider whether this person is the right fit for you.

Why not leave? Why not say, "Something in our marriage is missing and I want out?" The answer is complicated.

There are many reasons why a person does not leave. In my experience, the answer is never a simple, straightforward one.

While I do not have all the answers, I realize that I should have left a long time ago, but healing from abuse in any form is a process that cannot be rushed. To make such a permanent decision requires an understanding and recognition of the problem; clarity of who you are, what you want, and where you are going; and the re-establishment of boundaries so you never again lose yourself.

The bottom line is that those who are unfaithful have found themselves in a most difficult quandary. They are torn between honoring the commitment to their spouse and God, and trying to find a way to dull the ache that grows inside them. I have learned that shielding your heart from the pain will only keep the pain coming until you learn the lesson that it is trying to teach.

The truth is that if we follow our hearts, they will guide us to peace.

Chapter 38

Leaving – Indecision

No matter how hard I try, how much I give, or how much I think, I cannot bring back what is gone. I often lie in bed at night, looking at Liam, thinking about how great the good times were and how bad the tough times were. I recall the many nights I lay in bed, crying softly into my pillow, biting my lip so the sobs would not escape into the cool midnight air. I would wipe the tears away with the back of my hand, drying them in my soft down comforter, or stroke my hair to provide some sense of comfort.

I sometimes touch his face and wonder what it will be like to wake up without him next to me. How will I feel? How will he feel, knowing the pain he has caused me and our children?

Maybe he will be relieved to let go, and I will finally get some peace and much needed sleep.

As it stands right now, our marriage is over, and the future we were planning will never happen. I dread seeing the pain sweep across his face, when I say those cold, empty words. My heart aches at the thought; I cry just thinking about it. I can feel our shared pain so deeply already.

Though he no longer loves me, I provided him with stability. He would often tell me, in the early days of our marriage, how much he loved to come to bed and how often he would contrast it with sleeping in the barn. For him, one of life's simple pleasures is a warm bed.

For all that we have been through, I will miss him, honestly. I know that may be shocking, but deep down, he is a good man, who cannot help what life has done to him. Though there were tough times and struggles, there were other areas of our marriage where he demonstrated his kindness and thoughtfulness, but they did not outweigh the pain brought forth by his actions.

His choices were different from mine, and he let his insecurities get the better of him. I was hoping that, over time, he would learn to let go of the negative and focus on the positive, but the task was too challenging.

A quarter century is a long time to be with someone, to get to know them inside and outside, to adjust and create your own routines, to be able to predict their behavior. I do not know if I want to let go and start over; I do not know if I can, or if I have the strength to do so.

The thought of being alone, with no one to share my life, makes me sad, but thoughts of staying haunt me, and the thought of facing more abuse makes me grimace. I do not know if I could survive it. I barely survived the first twenty years, when I was happily unaware. What would the next twenty, thirty, or more be like?

As we struggle with our current circumstance, Liam continues to use his poor coping strategies. I do not want to deal with it because I view it as self-inflicted, controllable behavior..

I drown myself in work – ten to twelve hours a day, every day – to avoid going home, unable to bear the thought of what may happen when I get there.

When I do go home, I eat and sleep, clean the house, and do laundry when I must. My absence is hardly fair to my children, I know, but until I restore my strength, I cannot face it. I have to heal and repair myself.

I look for a solid, concrete reason to stay, without finding one. I try to convince myself that I should stay for the kids, but they are adults now, and I may have done them a disservice by staying this long.

I think about how much I dread being alone, but that is not a reason to stay. If he agreed to go to counselling and at least try, would I stay? Is that a reason? Or if we separated, would it offer Liam and I a chance at individual happiness?

Connor sums it up best. The only thing that would ever make me do something is love. Love matters. Sharing love, being in love, making love, matters to me. It is the entirety of who I am. I cannot endure a life without love. If I had not met Connor, I do not know what I would have done. I think I would be dead. I had been adrift at sea for so long that he became my shore, my home.

His love keeps me going, calms me, helps me bloom, and clears the cobwebs from my mind. It feeds my soul, heals my heart, and replenishes my well. Truly, his love is a gift of life.

At the end of the day, Connor, our love, what I feel in my heart, is significant. No matter how many times I think it through, the only choice is to leave.

While I cannot build a future on the uncertainty of Connor leaving his own marriage, I can build it on faith, trust in God, and in myself. When I take action to leave, it will be because it is what *I* want. The decision will be based on my survival, sanity, respect, dignity, and peace.

Chapter 39

Daniel – Again?

I was lying in bed, scrolling through my Facebook, when a message popped up. "Hi, baby, how are you?" I went to the messenger and there it was, a message from Daniel. *How did he find me? Should I respond?* A thousand thoughts ran through my head as my heart began pounding. The feelings from the past came rushing forward like a tsunami.

My hands shook as they texted, "I'm fine. How are you?"

It had been almost two full years. Why was he reaching out now?

"I miss you, baby. I love you so much."

My eyes rolled, *as if.* God, if he only knew how much I had wanted those words to be true years ago, how much I had needed his love to be real.

"Can I call you? Please, baby? I want to hear your voice."

Oh my. "Yes, fine, call me."

He was declaring his love for me, attempting to convince me of how much he missed and wanted me, how he had been searching everywhere to locate me.

What are you doing, Kate?

Connor immediately came to mind. *You have a man who loves you more than anything in this world, stop this foolishness*, I thought.

Daniel continued, "I love you, Kate. You are one in a

million."

Yes, I am, though you never knew it.

He was convincing, persuasive, and sounded sincere. Tears welled in my eyes as my voice cracked, telling him I had to go.

"Don't cry, baby. Now you have me crying." Daniel sent a picture of tears streaming down his face.

I messaged my friend. "Oh no! Kate, stay away from him. You know he is lying."

She was right. In my heart, I did know. I could not listen to his lies any more. *Oh, dear God, help me.*

He called day and night for two weeks, until finally, strength came and courage appeared.

"The woman you loved – the sweet, innocent, naïve woman – the kind, generous, and loving woman – she died. She died of a broken heart, of loneliness and starvation from a lack of love, and she almost literally died. She can never go through that again. Ever. Daniel, you don't love me. You need me. There is a difference," I texted him.

It was the most incredible moment of freedom. I realized that I loved the *illusion* of him, and what I wanted him to be – my prince, my savior, my Mr. Fix-My-Life. I breathed a sigh of relief and sent him a final text: "I wish you well. Please find yourself a woman who loves you and have a happy life. It has taken a while, but I am moving on. Please do not contact me again."

I exhaled. It was over, I had closure.

He sought my kindness, and I gave it freely, but I have learned that I cannot continue to give away my most precious gift, my love. I meant it, I can never go through that again.

I will never again be an enabler, deny my needs, or put the needs of others ahead of my own. That path will never be travelled again; I could not survive it.

The problem with being a person who loves so deeply and cares so much is that I do not know when to stop giving and loving. If there is anything I have learned, it is that kind people must have boundaries, because takers do not know when to stop taking.

Ravaged and left for dead, I had nothing left in me to give. Scarily, I did almost die, by my own hand, because I did not think I had the strength and perseverance to keep going.

Connor picked me up, carried me away, and healed me. He filled my well with more love than I could have ever hoped or asked for. Thanks to him, I am alive; I am healing and getting stronger. He saved me, in more ways than I can express, and he helped me find the means to save and heal myself. He is my life, my rock, my best friend, and my confidante. He is my strength – him, and God. With God, I can do anything; I can live and love again.

Chapter 40

Grieving

I laugh when I think of the many people who have told me, "You are so lucky, you have it all." If they only knew. I do not have it all. I am holding myself together with a one-inch piece of twine and a chewed-up piece of bubble gum. Aren't we all?

No one has it all, no matter how they present themselves. Some of us are better actors, able to make you believe what we want you to believe. We have learned mechanisms to cope, hide the pain, and smile through the tears, our scars invisible to the human eye. That is, until the day arrives when life hits you squarely in the jaw, and you cannot fake it any more.

"Are you okay?" is the worst possible question you can be asked when you're on the brink of collapse. Your mind screams "no" while your lips betray you, and you quickly respond, "Yes, I'm fine thanks. How are you?" You fear that the waves of grief will overwhelm you, giving truth to your reality. And the smile – the bright, radiant, captivating smile – that erupts from the corners of your mouth can convince even the most cynical sceptic that you are, in fact, fine.

Grieving is a natural part of the healing process, and heaven knows I had a lot to grieve. I thought I was well on the road to better mental health when the grieving process kicked in unexpectedly after the death of my beloved dog.

I was in a meeting when the waves of sadness arrived. I

excused myself and headed to the washroom to calm myself and splash cool water on my face.

That's when it happened. My friend stopped me in the corridor and asked if I was ok. The dam broke, spilling the tears I had contained in a downpour over my face. She hugged me, making it worse, as I politely excused myself and ran the rest of the way to the washroom to regain my composure.

She must have called me a dozen times after that moment, to check on me, asking if there was anything she could do, or any way she could help me.

Once I started to cry, I could not stop. For the next two months I cried all the time – for anything and everything. In the hallways at work, in my office in front of friends and colleagues, even at home.

I was so embarrassed. I didn't know how to respond, unprepared for the onslaught of questions that followed. Colleagues and acquaintances were concerned for my well-being, offering comfort and support, uncertain of why I was upset.

Liam had never seen me in such a state, and he was exceptionally nice to me. "I hate seeing you so sad. Cheer up, things will get better."

I was grieving for so much – the loss of my son's normal life, my foster daughter, my marriage, my mom's illness, the lost promotion, the loss of my dog, and the loss of myself. I was grieving for the times when I had loved everyone so much that I forgot about loving me; for giving away so much of myself that I had nothing left to love me. I grieved for thinking I could have it all and do it all, without recognizing my own limitations. I grieved because no one loved me the way I loved them.

I took two weeks off work to recuperate, but it was not

enough.

Being a boss is not easy, especially if you are a softie like me. Known for being a compassionate, empathetic manager, I always took other people's problems on as my own and tried my best to help guide them toward resolution.

The problem with being empathetic and sympathetic as a boss is that no one understands the reasons for your decision making, and you are unable to share this knowledge with them because of privacy and confidentiality policies. Unaware of the extenuating circumstances surrounding some situations, staff judge you, asserting that you are too harsh or too soft, in a mood or inflexible. It is impossible to please them or to make them understand.

In many cases, staff would never be able to see beyond their purview to consider the reasons why I or other staff behaved as we did. Complaining about trivial matters made me want to dismiss their complaints, because in the big scheme of things, they were petty and childish. If everyone did their work, I did not care that X came in late or that Y was late returning from lunch because they needed to feed their elderly parent.

I understand that there is a boundary between your personal and professional life, but sometimes the lines blur, and that is unavoidable. Not everyone has a support system to assist in such matters, and common sense must prevail.

Feeling mentally, physically, and emotionally drained, and unable to cope with staff bellyaching, I stayed home and listened to music, walked on the treadmill, slept a lot, and fell into a state of depression. I stayed there for quite a while.

Avoidance and adrenaline – for the next several months, those were my strategies. Do not think about the pain, avoid thinking about the future, and live on adrenaline. For the record, it is an extremely poor strategy. It simply makes you more tired. I thought I was ready to move on, but I was not.

The world was too much to deal with, and I did not want to feel the ache. I knew I had to come to terms with life and my decisions, though, because it is the only way to heal.

The worst part was being unable to verbalize why I was upset I felt that no one would understand the loss I felt, the lack of control, or the finality of my life as I knew it. No one could see the scars on my heart or feel the pain in my soul.

I could not pretend any more. I did not want to hide; I wanted to be free from the expectations, the demands, and the responsibilities so I could be myself. I wanted to stop the sense of desperation and loneliness I felt every day and replace it with happiness.

Chapter 41

The Best Laid Plans (Damn COVID)

I do not know what it is with me and the universe, but someone or something out there just does not like me. You know what they say about the best laid plans…

I watched the news and shook my head. Connor and I had agreed to meet, to affirm that our feelings were real, and everything came to a screeching halt because of COVID-19.

I knew Connor would never approve of my travelling during the pandemic. He would never allow me to put myself in harm's way, and I felt the same. It was simply too risky. We were both middle-aged with an elevated risk of infection. We would simply have to ride out the storm and pray for a fast recovery. It was March 2020. *This will probably be a few months*, I thought. *I can do this. I have survived everything else, what is one more hurdle?*

The one good thing about lockdown was that it offered time to ruminate and ensure that Connor and this new life were what I wanted. This time, there was no rush, no pressure, and no family expectations. We were both old enough to make decisions regarding our happiness and future without interference from the outside world.

As I reflected on the past year, I realized that my emotional affair was impacting many people – Liam, Connor, Maeve, our families, and our friends. I had no right to think only of myself. If I was not able to make up my mind, I should leave and sort it out.

Fear was making me stay. Fear of change, of what my family would think, how my children would react, and of being alone. I was trying to have my cake and eat it too.

Breaking the cycle of abuse takes an incredible amount of strength and courage. Whatever was to happen, I needed to figure it out without influence from anyone. Although terrified, it did not change the fact that I cared for someone other than my husband. That one point was the reason I needed to walk out the door. Everything else was an excuse, or a reason to convince myself to stay.

Time away from Connor, and the clamor of the world, offered time for clarity and serenity. I did not want to rush into another relationship. I needed to be sure that there were no doubts, hesitations, or concerns. If there were, meeting Connor would have to wait.

Meanwhile, things at home had calmed, and everyone had a new focus. Liam stepped up – cooking, cleaning, doing the laundry, and taking care of the kids – relieving some of the pressure because, by the time I came home from work, I simply had no energy to do anything.

I did not have a single complaint about him. He never once degraded me, insulted me, or instigated an argument, and though it was odd, it was also a relief. He stopped drinking and smoking; I assume it was out of fear that he would contract the virus and die.

One Saturday morning, we were lying in bed, and I could hear the thud of his heart against his chest. "Do you want to be here?" he sputtered.

I froze like a deer caught in the headlights, not expecting the question. "Why do you ask?" I responded quizzically.

With his eyes focused on mine, he replied, "Because, for the past few years, you have made me feel like you don't care if I live or die."

Without thinking, I blurted out, "Well, that's ironic! That is exactly how you've made me feel for the last twenty years."

Silence and shock ensued for both of us. This was a breakthrough. If there was ever a time for honesty, it was that moment. For the next hour or more, we discussed everything that ached inside us.

He outlined how he was afraid to approach me, uncertain of my reaction and apologized for driving me over the edge.

I told him that his behavior had destroyed my soul, crushed my spirit, and ruined my belief in love. "I do not know if there is a way to save this marriage. You have always treated me poorly, never as your wife, the woman you are supposed love and cherish."

I explained how we lacked support, tenderness, communication, and affection; all things that should exist between married couples. Holding nothing back, we poured out our souls and the mountains of emotions inside each of us.

His response was that he loves me more than anything in the world, but he has been battling his own demons and was unable to give me what I desperately needed.

Later, as he stepped in the shower, I lay quietly in our bed. I stared at the sunshine beyond the white wooden blinds, the tapping of water on the shower door drowning out and overpowering my thoughts. His final words echoing in my head, "*If the marriage fails, I will accept my role in its demise.*" It was one of the few times he took responsibility for his actions.

I do not know why I did not end it that day. It was the perfect opportunity, but something deep inside of me was not ready to let go. It made me wonder if, in this process of death and rebirth, God was not only transforming me, but Liam too.

Chapter 42

Resolution and Peace – 2022

They say that time heals all wounds, and I suppose that is true, but wounds create scars that can never be undone. No one gets off the ride of life until death, so we learn to make the best of it.

Despite the madness, time brought resolution and peace, as it does with most events.

Mom and Dad divorced twenty years after their initial separation. Now, twenty years after their divorce, they are living in the same household again. With Mom unable to care for herself, Dad does her grocery shopping and helps around the house. Life is full of twists and turns. Love remains a mystery.

Mya and I continue to live our individual lives with our families. While we may not be as close as we once were, we are no longer as distant as we have been. Nothing can erode the bond of love between sisters.

William, James, and I have renewed our close relationship. Conversation and communication are the keys to unlocking all that ails you.

One evening, William came to the kitchen get a glass of water and inquired why I was writing at such a late hour. I took advantage of the moment and shared with him.

"My counsellor says it is a great technique to clear your head. I find it helpful."

"Your counsellor?" he asked curiously.

I briefly explained how sad and confused I had been over the past few years, and the toll life was taking on me. Initially, he seemed aloof, but once I told him that I was simply trying to love everyone the best way I could, he dropped his guard, and I seized the moment.

"William, I love you more than you will ever know. I am not perfect. I did not have all the answers. In the moment, I tried to do what was right, and in hindsight, I made some poor decisions. But I am human, and we all make mistakes. What you learn from the mistakes is what you need to focus on. I will never let anyone or anything come between you and me, or James and me, ever again."

Without missing a beat, he jumped up and hugged me. "I love you, Mom."

One conversation renewed our close relationship, and another piece of my soul healed. The bond of love between a mother and her child is unbreakable.

James graduated high school, obtained his driver's license, found a job, and began his first semester in university. Though he will remain partially paralyzed for the rest of his life, he is grateful for the sensations and aspects of life that he has regained. I wish him happiness as he continues his journey toward a positive and constructive future. He has been a source of hope and inspiration to me, never letting life detract from his joy. Together, we have grown to be stronger and more resilient, learning to persevere through life's trials. Change is not the end, but the beginning of a new path.

Amanda finished high school, obtained her driver's license, and is actively employed. She lives with her extended family, and we remain close. In my eyes, she will always be the daughter I never had, and my love for her will never change. I am her support system, as any parent is for their child, and I intend to remain her foster mother for years to come. As she battles her demons, she is learning to love and care for herself, and I pray that God supports her during her trials.

Edward remains my boss and we continue working together, despite our fractured relationship. While I can acknowledge that he pushed me outside of my comfort zone and forced me to grow, I may never trust him again. However, I have learned to understand him and the importance of being kind.

Ironically, time has shown that he was battling his own demons and living with his own abuse. Confiding in each other and sharing our stories was a turning point in our relationship. Two souls battling the same demons at the same time. Who could have known? Nothing is ever as it seems.

George, my work colleague, and I continue to work together, and we have built and completed several significant projects that benefited the organization. We remain friends, and he is still my sounding board and my guide through turbulent waters.

The lesson George taught me about momentum applies to my personal life too; never wait for something to be perfect. Each step, no matter how small, is propelling you closer to your goals. Just when you think you've reached perfection, there is more change, fears, and uncertainty, and you begin anew.

George has also taught me that kindness and generosity are wonderful traits to have, but some people are never satisfied because they live with an ungrateful heart. His positive influence in my life and my thought process has been a blessing.

Managers have thankless jobs, and staff often forget that they are human and have their own problems and issues. Be kind and show them the empathy and sympathy you expect for yourself.

Learning how to control your emotions when dealing with staff, and making rational decisions while being disrespected, is a super trait; appreciate those who possess it.

Six years later, my doctor friend and I continue hug therapy. Our friendship has spanned the thirty-year course of my career, and I am eternally grateful for his generous emotional support. His devilish grin and good looks still make me stammer, though, somehow, I have learned to successfully string sentences together and appear coherent. My face however continues to betray me with its bright crimson color.

I never heard from Daniel again.

Mona and I remain friends. He has lost his entire family now and depends on me like a mother. It is a role to which I am better suited.

My friends are a blessing, riding out the storms with me and providing shelter, support, and comfort when I need it. Loving others has always been my strength.

Connor has forever changed me, making it impossible for me to be the same person I once was. Somehow, by helping me find and restore my missing pieces, he helped me to define a softer, more tender, beautiful version of myself. My deep-rooted pain has been replaced with a sense of hope and assurance for the future.

Despite my plans and dreams for taking steps toward the new me and a new life, the universe has its own plans. I remain home with Liam, and Connor remains home with Maeve; we are unable to be together because of world events. True love remains elusive.

Chapter 43

Lessons Learned – 2022

I have invested heavily in myself over these past few years. I have learned that what people dislike the most about change is the fear of what the future holds for us. Do not be afraid to start over, no matter where you are in your life.

Stepping out of your safe, predictable comfort zone will bring unexpected rewards, and it is the only way to grow. Take the risk and invest in yourself, it is worth the time and effort; nothing is more valuable.

I am defined by the terms and limitations I put on myself, not by my past or what people think of me. If I believe I can, *I can*. Learn to trust yourself and believe in your ability. Every obstacle in my path has provided an opportunity to learn, change directions, or start fresh. I have made it this far by the grace of God; He will not forsake me now, He never does.

The journey of the past few years has been a blessing. God never brings pain without purpose. He will guide my steps to where I am supposed to go, even if, to me, it feels like I am stumbling down the wrong road. Somehow, I will end up where I need to be, and with the man for whom I am destined. How it unfolds is in the hands of my savior.

When I recently walked across the stage to collect my parchment for my master's degree, thirty-two years after I received my bachelor's degree, the sense of pride I exuded was overwhelming. I was proud of myself because this accomplishment was mine alone. Mom and I still cried, but this time we were crying together for the same reason. You are never too old to fulfil your dreams.

Education is a means to propel yourself forward; use it to your advantage and create forward momentum. Educate yourself in academic and non-academic subjects; you can never be too educated.

Despite COVID wreaking havoc with my schedule, I have returned to the gym, resumed healthy eating, and restarted my lifestyle change. With time, effort, discipline, and determination, I am becoming a happier and healthier version of myself.

Love will make you do some crazy things, whether it is staying with an abuser, having an affair, or changing your behavior so radically that you are unrecognizable. Stay true to yourself, let no one change you from the person you were meant to be. Be honest with yourself, only you know what you truly desire, no one can make that decision for you.

Keeping your wits about you while in love is necessary for your survival. Never give so much of yourself to another person that you have nothing left for yourself.

As women, we need to take time for ourselves, and we need to make ourselves a priority. We not only deserve it but need it.

If we constantly give so much of ourselves away, we will become depleted, and we are of no use to ourselves or anyone when there is nothing left to give.

We need to know our worth, express our authenticity, and understand the value we add to this life. It is something that, as women and mothers, we need to learn and teach.

Each one of us has value. We are a puzzle piece created to fit somewhere in life's journey, and no one else fits where we do.

Each one of us is a gift to the world, and we need to listen to the voice telling us which path to choose and drown out those voices saying we can't, or aren't enough, because *we are enough*. God created us to be enough. We would never be tasked with this life if we were unable to complete it.

Speak kindly to yourself. Learn to love who you are and what you offer this world. There is only one you.

Happiness is a conscious decision that must be chosen every day; let nothing and no one deter you from it.

Infidelity is not right in any circumstance, even mine. I wrote this to explain my behavior, the grief and loss I was suffering, the abuse and hardships I endured, and the loss of myself, but it does not excuse it. I hope that, by sharing my story, I help you understand the complex, unimaginable, and unexpected path to infidelity.

I should have left many years ago, and, perhaps, I should never have married; but you cannot cry over spilled milk, you can only learn from it. The decisions and choices we make throughout our lives are never easy, and those made at one moment in time may not seem appropriate years later. Hindsight is always 20/20.

Take your time when choosing a life partner; there is no rush. Their significance in your life cannot be understated. Have faith that love will find you when it is meant to, and do not jump into marriage just because your friends have found happiness. Love is patient and kind, I am certain of that. The person who is meant to love you will find and wait for you.

Acceptance of your actions and their consequences is necessary for forgiveness and understanding. Accountability for your actions makes you grow as an individual. My desire to have children and my choice of spouse led me to this path, and I accept the consequences and the lessons that accompany them.

Many of us have made decisions based on loneliness or fear, or to please others. The consequences of such decisions can be far-reaching, affecting people who are not in our range of view at that time. If your heart tells you "no," trust it. It may be painful in the moment, but it will hurt much less than when children are involved, or others whose hearts do not deserve to be impacted by your decisions.

One of the most beautiful things I have learned on this journey is how resilient I am, and women are in general. We laugh, cry, cuss, get angry, and yet somehow, dust ourselves off and keep going. We are designed to overcome life's challenges and survive, regardless of the obstacles placed in our path.

Most importantly, always know that no matter how bad it is today, there is always tomorrow. Never give up or lose hope, even in the storms. For after every storm, no matter how long it lasts, comes better weather.

Chapter 44
Till Death Do Us Part

The realization Connor and I could never be together weighed heavily on my mind. Despite the love we shared, the physical closeness we craved would never become reality.

Death became an unconscious focus of my daily life because it seemed more appealing than my current existence. We had talked about the afterlife many times, and I remembered him saying, "When I die, throw our ring into the ocean. It is there in the depths where we met, and it is there where we shall meet again."

The sun was warm and inviting as I sat by the seaside in my car and twirled the *Mo Anam Cara* ring on my finger, as I stared at my phone and kissed his picture one last time. If I could not have him in the physical realm, then I would wait for him in death. At least there we could be together.

It was a beautiful day. I had written letters to my children, husband, parents, sister, and friends, and placed them carefully on the seat where they could be found when needed. I smiled to myself and placed the car keys safely under the mat and walked slowly and intentionally toward the water.

The waves crashed against the shoreline, the riptide beckoning for me to dip my feet in, to carry me away. Though I could not see my destination, I walked deliberately in his direction confident this was the only way. As the waves washed over my body, I cried out, "I love you."

Ashes to ashes and dust to dust, looking for that blessed hope…

It was fast and painless. Ripped apart by the currents, pieces of my physical body shredded like my soul, carried away in the waves of the cold north Atlantic Ocean to the shores of Ireland, where I could finally be with the man I loved. I did not throw the ring in between us; I threw myself instead.

As the months passed, Connor grieved for me, his soulmate, bereft with my absence and warmth. One day, while walking along the shoreline, a single ray of sunshine landed on the murky path reflecting upward, catching Connor's attention. He stopped to investigate, picking up the muddy object, rinsing it in the water.

He stared in awe: the *Mo Anam Cara* ring.

I made it home. I was finally at peace.

Gasping and breathless, I was jolted awake. I leapt out of bed, my heart pounding. That dream felt a little too real.

I calmed myself and regained my bearings. *No. This will not be how my story ends. I have come too far.* I refuse to let life alter who I am.

My soul softly whispered, "Then it's time."

Epilogue

It ended with a sigh. Liam was being kind and thoughtful, and I hoped the man I had married and loved was transformed.

Two weeks later, he demeaned and degraded me again. He proceeded to the front door, unaffected by his words, as I stood in silence. There was no need to respond. I hung my head, my shoulders dropped, and I knew he had crossed the boundary that I had just reinstated.

I departed for work, and when comfortably seated in the car, I exhaled and texted him. "I want to separate."

"I know. I've known for a while," he responded.

Benjamin Franklin was right, you can do anything if you put your mind to it, even if that means starting a new chapter of your life and putting a line through the years that came before it.

Twenty-five years of marriage, over; not with an argument, drama, screaming, or yelling, but with a simple four-word sentence. It was done.

I scanned the horizon as I drove away, my eyes filled with tears. Everything would be okay. The war within me and between us was finally over, and somehow, I had lived to tell the tale.